Public Library Pioneer

Keith McClellan

Contents

Street Map of Part of Tottenham

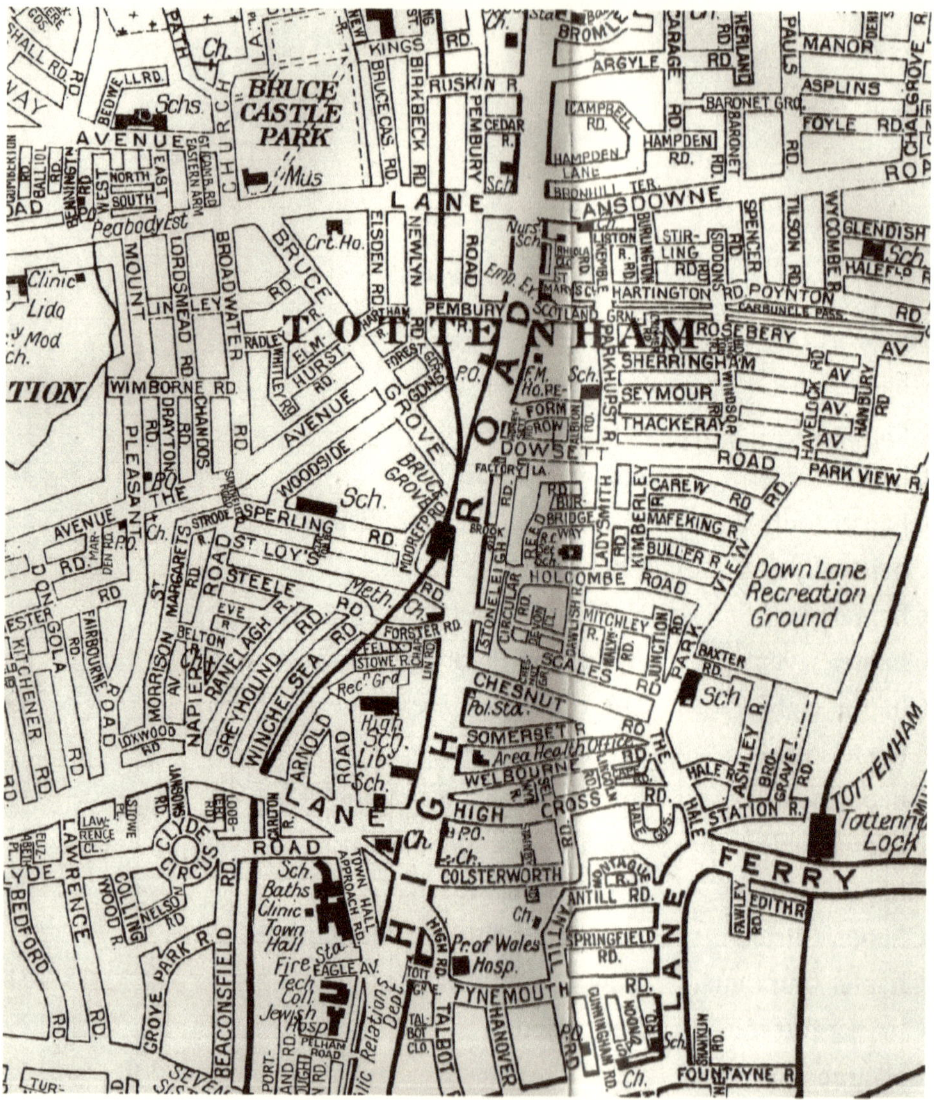

The Risley Avenue School is just on the top left of the map under Bedwell Road. Lordship Lane runs along the base of Bruce Castle Park.

Other areas clearly marked are Antill Road, Greyhound Road, Rosebery Avenue, Seymour Avenue and Parkhurst Road School.

A. W. McClellan

"From the time I first appreciated the deeper significance of libraries in our society I wanted to inspire, if I could, this same significance among my colleagues working in the library. It seemed to me that the library stood for so much that those who worked in it should, consciously or unconsciously, absorb into their personal working relationships that same spirit, if they were to be effective." A. W. McClellan, extract from letter to former staff member.

".... a man with ideas who, unusually, put them into practice, tested and proved them. I was impressed by the logic and clarity of his exposition. ..... He was ahead of his time in advocating connecting to, and learning from, the communities served by the library." Wendy Spinks.[1]

"McClellan was a man of vision and a pioneer who developed a strategic method before the means existed to efficiently put it into practice. I advocate that his anticipation of, and contribution to, later developments deserves acknowledgement and a place in the library and information science 'Hall of Fame'." Wendy Spink.

"He was one of the outstanding librarians of his age..."Philip Colehan, Borough Librarian, London Borough of Hillingdon, p165, Lib Assoc Record, 87 April 1985.

"Had he been the chief of one of the more fashionable library systems, his fame would have been more publicly acknowledged, nationally and internationally." A. G. S. Enser, Borough Librarian, Eastbourne, Sussex, p. 121,Lib Assoc Record ,87. March 1985

These quotations, selected from a range of sources spread over a period from 1966 to 2010, convinced me that my father, A. W. McClellan, was more than just the family treasure he had always been; more than just a successful, hardworking professional librarian. He was an original thinker and innovator who fought for his ideas, based as they were on deeply held principles and well researched theories and practices. As he stated in the development plan he presented to the Libraries and Public Buildings

---

1 Wendy Spink is a Research Officer at Age UK. She wrote the article from which these quotes are taken for the Library Heroes column of the Library and Information Gazette, 25thMarch 2010.

Committee when he was appointed as Director of Public Libraries and Museum for the London Borough of Tottenham, the plan had been put together in some haste, but the principles it represented were the result of a great deal of thought and experience based upon his twenty years working in public libraries.

During my own professional life I was content to accept him as a caring father and family man. As a result, it is only by looking back over many years that I can see him in the wider context. Thus I was led to try to understand his work more fully and to investigate, to the best of my ability, the experiences in his life which had influenced the formulation of his theories and his skill in putting them into practice.

Through detailed research I discovered just how great a pioneer he was in shaping the modern public library. However, I was also anxious to convey the wonderful, loving family man he was. I relied on memories and based these parts of his story on imagined or partly remembered conversations, in the spirit of what I had experienced in the forty years or so we shared.

ARCHIBALD WILLIAM McCLELLAN

Chapter One

Growing up in Tottenham
"A hard-working and earnest little lad."

"You are the man of the house now, Archie," his father had said, "Look after your mother and Stuart and little Jackie, work hard at school and be a good boy. Ask Grandpa Parsons or one of your uncles if you need any help. I'll write whenever I can."

In the new year of 1917 Archie was eight and a half years old. By the 10th January his paternal grandfather had died of a short illness, his father had resigned his job as a fitter and workshop foreman to join the war effort, and his mother had given birth to his baby brother.

"But, Daddy, do you have to go?"

"It's my duty, son. You wouldn't want your friends to call me a coward, would you?"

"No, Daddy," said Archie.

So it's happened at last, he thought. He'd heard the arguments, especially after Uncle Sid had died in France. His dad had signed up at the last minute under something he called the Derby Scheme. He didn't have much choice, he'd said. That was over a year ago, but now he'd given up his job and done his basic training.

"Mummy, is Daddy going to France where Uncle Sid was killed?" he asked later, while his mother nursed the baby.

"No, son, he's off to Mesopotamia. He's going to mend the army lorries so they can drive through the desert."

"Are there Germans there?"

"No, it's their friends, the Turks."

"How long will he be away? Will he stay there till the war's over?"

"I expect so. Now, no more questions. Poor little Jackie needs to get some sleep."

He wanted to ask about smallpox and stories about soldiers dying there. He'd heard his parents arguing about vaccinations and being sent to the desert as a death sentence, but he kept that to himself.

It had all been so exciting when the war broke out. Soldiers and recruits marching up the street; all the young men, like his uncles, Sid and Stan, signing up; everyone convinced it would all be over by Christmas. He'd been worried when a big crowd of people attacked the jeweller's at the end of Dowsett Road, a few doors away from where his granddad and grandma lived. Mr Smith was a German, apparently, but his daddy said the Smiths had been there as long as he could remember. Anyway, his mummy had walked him to school in Parkhurst Road after that, to see him safe beyond the junction with Dowsett Road. Since then he had become more and more worried about the war, and of his daddy having to go. Food was short, so they sometimes went hungry, and quite often he'd see men in blue uniforms; men with horrible injuries. Some had broken arms; others, with no legs, were pushed along in wheelchairs. The ones that made him feel ill had burnt faces; little narrow eyes, no eyelids and puffy scarred cheeks; some had no real nose, or missing ears.

Another worry was the bombs dropping. Zeppelins, which looked to him like great big cigar-shaped balloons, flew over and dropped bombs on houses and factories. Sometimes the policeman came down the road on his bike. He would blow his whistle and shout, "Take cover," but most people didn't take any notice. He wished he knew how to make a bomb to get back at them.

Meanwhile, Archie continued to do his best at Parkhurst Road Boys' School. Many of the other boys had fathers and brothers away at the war. Most were in the trenches in France, so Archie felt a bit special with a dad in Mesopotamia. The other boys knew almost nothing of the Expeditionary Force, so he talked quite a lot about his Uncle Stanley, who lived next door with Auntie Emmie, and who had been on the Western Front, but was now in India. His mum and Auntie Emmie spent a lot of time together. Auntie Emmie had two little children not much older than his brother, Jackie. Sometimes one or other of the mums would look after all the children while the other one went shopping or on some other errand. He loved Auntie Emmie; she wasn't as strict as his mum and told him all about Uncle Stan's adventures in the war.

Life was hard on the home front in Tottenham, with food and fuel limited and expensive. Archie's father had given up a good job as foreman of the machine shop at the Liquid Air and Rescue Syndicate Ltd in Willesden, where he was valued for his competence and reliability. Tottenham was growing rapidly before the First World War. People were moving from other parts of London and, increasingly, from further afield, as factories were being built on the cheaper land by the marshes in the Lea Valley. Housing for the workers was spreading to match.

A music hall was built in 1908 and a skating rink was added a year later. With railway yards and new civic buildings, parts of the borough gave the feel of an urban centre. Yet as a series of paintings by John Bonny showed, there was much that remained rural.

Archie's father wrote regularly to his wife, the letters taking up to three months to arrive. It was clear that he missed the family, always asking after the boys and asking his wife, Nellie, to get Archie to write to him. His brother Stuart was nearly five when Archie first began to write to his father. Stuart was an irritating little boy at that age but Archie tried not to bully him. He had promised his daddy he would look after him, so he did his best. He didn't realise how long his letters would take to reach his father, so when his first special page arrived from Mesopotamia, with his mother's regular letter, he was delighted.

6/5/18 From Daddy

Dear Archie,

Just a few lines in answer to your welcome letters I am pleased you are all alright at home, and that you have been good boys and are getting on at school, now you must try and win that scholarship, ask mummy if you want to know anything, if she doesn't know ask granddad he will tell you. You must also try and learn the piano, by the time I get home, and then I can hear you play, Well Sonny I am sending you a photo of some Arab children so you can see what they are like out here, also one for Stuart now don't destroy them and I will try and get you some more. Well son I don't know of anything to tell you only that I am very pleased to hear you and Stuart and dear little Jackie are alright and thanks for writing, so now close with love to you all from your loving Daddy

XXXXX	*XXXXX*	*XXXXX*
Archie	*Stuart*	*Jackie*

He was pleased his father wanted him to pass his scholarship and he redoubled his efforts at school. His report in the summer of 1918 placed him 3rd out of 51 pupils, commended him on his effort, but added that he showed carelessness at times. If he was to get that scholarship, he would have to take more care with his work.

The war was over in the November of that year and the family waited anxiously for their father's return. In his letters in August and October, he had anticipated coming home in the near future. The rumours of the desert as death sentence resurfaced in Archie's mind. They heard no more until a letter sent in March 1919 from Rawalpindi. Archie's letter from the previous November had only just reached him as he had been transferred to the North West Frontier, where he chanced to meet Uncle Stan.

Archie's letters were full of his latest ideas and projects. He usually sent a list of words he wanted his father to explain the meaning of. He would also ask about electrical and general engineering. As the war drew to an end he wrote,

Daddy, I know how to make a bomb to get the Germans with. I've got all the chemicals and I'm going to make a really big one.

His father does his best to reply to a long list of engineering questions Archie has posed him and, in the following letter, sent a month later, he wrote,

If you can only do what you say, that you can read a micrometer and Vernier thoroughly you ought to make a good engineer. Well sonny, you say you want me to teach you when I come home, well all I can say is if you keep on as you are going, you will be able to teach me something in figures at any rate.

Archie's interest in chemical engineering caused his father some nervous amusement. In the same letter he wrote,

Well what about this bomb of yours, don't get blowing the house up with it as I want somewhere to come home to.

The experiment was irresistible, in spite of his increasing opposition to the whole concept of war. He had mixed a heap of the constituents of gunpowder on his bedroom floor and put a match to it as an experiment. It was not compressed so it did not explode, but burnt a hole through the floor to the room below. The resulting punishment ended any lingering interest in the trappings of war.

"I hate the war, Mum," he said, "and I'm going to join the Youth Group at the Quakers when I leave Parkhurst Road."

"You be careful, son. Those people can get you into trouble. Grown men who wouldn't go to the war are called traitors. They get put to death."

"Quakers don't; they were allowed not to go. The ladies there told me."

"We'll see what your Daddy has to say when he gets home. The war is over now, anyway," said his mum. Archie did start to go to the Quaker meetings, but was still happy to celebrate the peace at the street party at the end of term in July 1919. He had a commemorative cup and saucer, and a lead medallion, to celebrate victory, although his father was still away in India.

His father returned home and was demobilised at the beginning of 1920, in time to encourage Archie to win a scholarship to Risley Avenue Central School for Boys. His final report from Parkhurst Road congratulated him on his success. His class teacher described him *as a hard-working and earnest little lad whom it is a pleasure to teach.*

He attended Risley Avenue for four years, passing Cambridge Local Junior and Senior Examinations, before finishing his schooling in July 1924.

On his departure his headmaster, J. H. Williams, wrote,

I can speak most highly of him in every way. His conduct has been exemplary; he has made admirable use of the various opportunities the school provides and he has entered heartily into all the various activities of school life. I recommend him with great confidence as a trustworthy and persevering worker.

During this time, Archie's father had found well-paid employment as workshop manager for the Admiral Bus Company, which, in 1924, became the London Public Omnibus Company. His father was promoted to depot manager. In 1923, his mother gave birth to a baby girl they named Joyce Mary. The younger brothers were at elementary school. Stuart was doing well and preparing for the scholarship to follow his brother to Risley Avenue. Archie had developed a susceptibility to very painful boils on the back of his neck. The stiff collars, required at school, rubbed on the tender areas and spread the infection. His mother bathed them with disinfectant but they were persistent and left scars on his neck. He was to be troubled with them beyond adolescence, particularly at times of stress.

In the summer holidays, after leaving Risley Avenue, he spent a week with a group of boys from the Quakers at a camp in Chesham, in Buckinghamshire. They met with other groups and had a most enjoyable break. Archie edited the journal, "A Red Letter Week" to which most of the boys contributed. On his return, he was employed in the office of the local Quaker charity organisation. He studied at a Tottenham Polytechnic evening class and, in the following April, he gained a certificate in English from the Royal Society for Encouragement of Arts, Manufacture and Commerce. He next found employment in a city export merchant's office.

For his summer break in 1925, he joined a group from the youth section of the 'No More War' movement on a cycle ride across Holland to meet similar groups there and demonstrate their demand for a peaceful world. This followed a march in London on the annual 'No More War Day' on the last weekend in July, the anniversary of the outbreak of The World War.

Chapter Two

A Career Begins

"The Libraries Committee of the Council invite applications from well-educated youths."

"They want a junior assistant at the library, I've just seen it in the *Herald*," Archie waved a copy of the *Tottenham and Edmonton Weekly Herald* at his parents.

"Get those wet boots and coat off, Archie," said his mother.

"Then come and sit down and tell us properly," added his father, taking a Navy Cut cigarette from his silver case and flicking his cigarette lighter.

Archie took off his coat by the back door and shook the raindrops from it. He slipped off his boots, grabbed the *Herald*, and came back into the living room. "Can I tell you now?" he said, waving the newspaper impatiently. His mother was bobbing Joyce up and down on her knee and the younger boys were chasing round the table.

"Stuart, go and do some studying; haven't you got some homework? You can't take that scholarship for granted, lad."

"It's the weekend, Daddy, and you told me to play with Jackie more."

"Don't argue with your father, Stuart. Now settle down, Jackie, and Archie will read you a story before you go to bed, won't you, Archie?"

"Of course, Mum. Now, can I tell you about this job?" He glanced at both his parents. "It'd be best if I read it to you. *'The Libraries Committee of the Council invite applications from well-educated youths,'*" he indicated himself, *"from sixteen to seventeen years of age, for the appointment of Junior Male Assistant. Applications on forms provided, together with copies of not more than three testimonials, to me at the Town Hall, not later than noon on Monday 16th November 1925 in an envelope endorsed 'Junior Assistant'.*

'The commencing salary (at 16) is £30 per annum, plus bonus, in accordance with the Council's scale of salaries (approximately £24).' Then it says you can get the application forms and so on from the Central Library[2]. What do you think?"

"It's a good steady job if you can get it. If you work at it, you can get some more qualifications and get promoted. Risley Avenue should stand you in good stead," said his dad.

---

2 *Tottenham and Edmonton Weekly Herald,* Friday November 6th 1925

"Is it what you want to do?" asked his mum.

"You know I love reading and books. I would love it. Learning how libraries work, being able to look things up, and borrow any books I want."

"You'd better get down to the library and get yourself an application form then," said his dad.

Ten young men were summoned to take an examination, from which seven were deemed worth calling for interview. Archie was one of two from Risley Avenue School to appear before the Books Staff Sub-Committee in the evening of 25th November. As they waited their turn, Archie tried to chat to his friend, Cecil, from school, but both of them were too nervous to say much.

"Archibald McClellan," said a voice from the committee room door. He stood. "This way, young man. Don't be nervous." The door closed behind him and he sat in the seat the chairman indicated.

"Good evening, Mr McClellan. I am Councillor Jackson, on my right is Mr Bennett, the chief librarian, and Councillor Fordyce, and on my left, Mr Buck, Mr Dubery and Mr Ferguson". Archie glanced along the line, feeling a surge of nervousness, as the members of the panel were named. They all seemed quite old, except Mr Bennett, who looked about the same age as his father. He wore a smart black suit and a navy blue tie. The councillors all seemed about sixty and wore well-filled waistcoats under their jackets. Several had watch chains visible, looping into waistcoat pockets. There were four ashtrays on the table in front of the panel. These contained several cigar butts, presumably from their preliminary discussions.

"Perhaps you could begin by telling us why you want to work in our library," continued Councillor Jackson.

"Well, Sir, I use the library a lot. I used it for my studies at the Tech. and I'm very keen on science and technical things, inventing things I mean, and I couldn't do without the library. They fascinate me, all these books."

"Mr Bennett, would you like to ask Mr McClellan some questions?"

"Thank you, Chairman. Now, young man, working here is not just a chance to borrow more books, you know. There's lots of work to do. Do you know what sort of work you would be doing?"

"Well, Mr Bennett, Sir, when I sent in my application I came and talked to one of the assistants, and he told me that it is best to study for the A. L. A. qualification. He told me I would have to know where to put books away, how to help people find what they want and how to issue books and take them back when people return them."

"You certainly showed some initiative in asking about the work." Mr Bennett looked along the panel to register his approval. "What else did the assistant tell you?"

"One thing that surprised me was that most libraries have their shelves closed, so borrowers have to ask the librarian to get the books for them. I think it's wonderful that the shelves are open here. I love thumbing through books looking for just what I need. You can still ask for help if you need it," said Archie. He continued to answer the panel's questions confidently until Councillor Jackson said, "And lastly, young McClellan, What is your final goal? Where do you see yourself in twenty years' time?"

"I hope I can take over from Mr Bennett when he retires," said Archie, to general friendly laughter from the panel.

"A fine ambition indeed," said Councillor Jackson. "Thank you, young McClellan. Now, wait outside until we have finished the interviews and made our decision."

"Thank you, Sir," said Archie, feeling momentarily relieved that the ordeal was over. After the final interview, all seven sat there, tension rising as they waited. After what seemed an hour the secretary appeared.

"Archibald McClellan, the committee would like to speak to you again. Come through now." Archie rose and moved towards the committee room; the other six boys looked at each other in dismay.

"The committee has decided to appoint you, McClellan. Congratulations. You interviewed very well. Let us hope the quality of your performance is reflected in your work"[3].

"Thank you, Sir. I'll do my best, Sir."

"I got the job, Dad! Mum! I got the job!" shouted Archie when he got home. "I start in December. I can't wait to get started," he added, full of excitement.

"Well done, Son." His father shook his hand. "Oh, come here, Archie," he said and gave him a big hug. "You see what you can achieve if you work hard, Stuart. Make sure you get that scholarship."

Archie soon settled into his new role and began studying to qualify as a professional librarian. In the spring of 1926, however, there was tension in the workplace. The economy was entering a slump; the much heralded 'land fit for heroes,' was exposed as a dream and workers in the coalmines, and

---

3 Report of Books Staff Sub-Committee to Libraries Committee, Tottenham District Council. Dec 1925.

other industries, were suffering increased unemployment and a reduction in wages. In early May, the General Strike broke out. In Tottenham, government posters appeared, offering protection for workers who defied their unions and returned to work. A shortage of Special Constables was also causing problems. The Tottenham Trades Unions Emergency Committee published a local strike bulletin, at a penny a copy, to keep people informed of local and national strike news. The District Council was a unionised organisation. Returns on union membership were put before the committee in June 1926 and all were registered members of N.A.L.G.O[4]. The library staff did not join the strike, although they did nothing to help resist its effects. Archie supported his father, whose workshop at the omnibus depot was almost deserted for the strike's duration.

Early in the year, the committee had responded positively to a proposal, from Poplar Library Committee, that discussions be held to consider the possibility of a joint municipal bindery. Since library books needed much more hardwearing bindings than books owned by individuals, the idea of a number of councils setting up a joint bindery seemed worth exploring. Tottenham already had a small bindery, to repair those books with covers damaged by heavy usage, but the idea of a number of councils combining in a larger bindery could well save on costs. In May, union representatives were quick to point out that binding involved twelve separate processes, each carried out by different people, for practical reasons as well as by trade union order. No agreement was reached and a recommendation was made to appoint one or more book repairers.[5] The rebinding of books remained an ongoing issue at Tottenham.

In the new year, 1927, Archie was summoned to the Librarian's Office.

"Well, McClellan; Archie; isn't it?" said Mr Bennett.

"Yes, Sir."

"I thought so; a good start to the New Year. You've passed your Library Routine[6] exam; one down and three to go, for your A.L.A. Well done and keep up the good work."

"Thank you, Sir. I'll do my best."

"Before you go, we have just appointed a new junior. Says he knows you from school. Preston, his name is, Walter Preston[7]. I see from your expression you know him."

---

4 Op. Cit. June 1926 . National Association of Local Government Officers
5 Minutes of Tottenham Public Libraries Committee, Feb & May 1926
6 Original L.A. Certificate. 6. Library Routine. Dec 1926.
7 Minutes of TPLC p118 Jan 1927

"Wally, yes Sir. He was two years below me so we didn't see a lot of each other."

"Keep an eye on him, would you? See he settles in and so on."

"I will, Sir. Thank you, Sir."

"Good lad. Now off you go; I'm sure you have a lot of work to do."

Archie came up behind the new recruit, who was preoccupied with sorting out returned books for replacing on the correct shelves.

"2LO calling, Walter, 2LO calling, Walter," he said.

"Archie McClellan," said Walter. He turned round and his face lit up. He reached forward and they shook hands, smiling at each other. He had looked up to Archie at school, as one of the most highly regarded pupils in the top class.

"Mr Bennett told me you worked here and were doing well."

"He's asked me to keep an eye on you," said Archie. "Make sure you keep up to the mark." He smiled. Walter smiled back uncertainly. "Don't worry, Wally, I'll help you all I can. I've just passed my first certificate, 'Library Routine', so I can help you with that, and show you the ropes generally."

"Thanks, Archie," he grinned. "How long have you been here?"

"Just over a year: I started before Christmas the year before last. Anyway, we can have more of a chat over tea and a smoke at the break. See you then," said Archie. Over time they became firm friends as well as colleagues. Archie, having led the way in the library qualifications, helped Walter as he prepared for each examination.

'2LO calling' had been a catch phrase among the schoolboys, four years previously, after the first public broadcast by the British Broadcasting Company had so caught their imagination. They would open every conversation with '2LO calling, 2LO calling'. Before long, there were little build-your-own wireless shops dotted along the High Road. Fathers had been to the Post Office to purchase a licence and crystal sets were carefully assembled. A year later, the *Radio Times* was published for the first time, listing the programmes for the week. Archie's love of all things mechanical - bicycles, motor cars and the buses his father worked on - as well as the arrival of electric light in streets, and some houses, was heightened even further at the prospect of the wireless.

"It's really annoying that the BBC chose Arsenal, of all clubs, for their football broadcast," said Archie at tea break. "Have you got a wireless, Wally?"

"My dad has. We listened to it during the strike. It's amazing really, how it's come on. Spurs should be on soon. They're bound to extend the coverage, aren't they?"

"I suppose so. I hope so anyway; I've built my own crystal set. I got a constructor's licence from the Post Office. I read it all up in the wireless mags, in the reference section. They have *Popular Wireless* and *Wireless World* and it tells you all the stuff you need, and what's best. I've got a Brownie and some headphones from Gammages. It works really well."

"I just read the *Radio Times* to see what's on," said Walter. "I can listen on our set at home if I want to."

Technology and mechanics were not Archie's only interests outside his work. After his march with the youth section of the 'No More War' movement, and his work in the charity shop, he continued his involvement with the Quakers. He had been ill at the end of March 1928,but, by the end of April, he was a key figure in an English concert, presented by the Tottenham Young People's Adult School. He chaired the concert and presented the first item, which he had written, and for which he had designed the stage set; *'The End of the World, A Reverie,'.* This finished with a rendering of *Jerusalem*. The first half ended with an item by local MP, R. C. Morrison, on *Our English Heritage*, and the concert ended with Community Singing and Auld Lang Syne.

Archie was particularly influenced by the ideas of Pierre Ceresole, a pacifist and Quaker, from Lausanne in Switzerland. Ceresole had been imprisoned on ten occasions, for refusal to pay tax for defence costs, and saw the Quakers as natural pacifists. He was clear that Pacifism would only attract support by doing practical work to help communities recover from disasters, man-made or natural. *'We need the firm rock of well-directed action if we are to resist the terrible drift, dragging us towards reactions of fear, hatred and violence.'*

His practical projects had begun with Austrian and German pacifists, joined by English, Dutch and Swiss volunteers, working in France to clear rubble and debris from war damage and building houses. The success of this gave him the *peacework technique*, as he called it. A project to help a Swiss community recover from an avalanche expanded the scheme.

The International Volunteers for Service organisation was formed. In 1928, it recruited 700 volunteers from 17 countries to help Lichtenstein recover from a burst dam on the Rhine, which led to the flooding of the whole country. It was as part of this volunteer force that Archie spent his annual leave, in the last week of May 1928.

In April 1929, a month before his twenty-first birthday, Archie was awarded Associate membership of the Library Association, having gained his fourth certificate. At this point he was Assistant-in-charge of the Central Reference Department.[8] His coming of age and professional qualification entitled him to promotion to a grade 'B' salary, as the librarian pointed out to the Library Committee.

During these years, the Library and Museum provision in Tottenham was expanding. Archie's original post had been created partly as a result of the opening of the Coombes Croft Branch. In 1929, plans were advanced for the opening of a new branch in Cissbury Road. Archie's promotion had been raised on the departure of an experienced Junior Assistant at the end of 1928. The Council and Staff Joint Committee had not met again by the following May. The librarian drew the overdue need for upgrading Archie to the attention of the Libraries and Museum Committee.[9]

By October, stock was being purchased for the new branch and the librarian pointed out that there was much work to be done before March of the following year, which was the estimated date for the new branch opening. In the light of this, he proposed that Junior Assistant H. A. Fellows be appointed as Assistant-in-charge of Cissbury Road, and A. W McClellan be promoted from Assistant-in-charge of the Central Reference Dept to Mr Fellows' current post as Assistant-in-charge of the Central Lending Department. with commensurate changes to follow.[10] The following month the committee decided to defer the decision and advertise the positions[11].

At the meeting of March 1930,[12] the committee finally agreed to the librarian's recommendations. As part of his promotion, Archie was to receive a £10 increase in salary without additional bonus. In the meantime, both men had become frustrated by the deferral and the decision to advertise, and had applied for a Senior Assistant Post in the Metropolitan Borough of Poplar.

Another cause of staff expansion of considerable interest to Archie, although not directly related to his duties, was the re-establishment of the museum at Bruce Castle. The castle was a 16th century manor house in Tottenham, which was acquired by the Hill family in 1827. The Hills

---

8 Minutes of TPLC p165 May 1929

9 Library and Museums Committee minutes May 1929, p165

10 Op Cit Oct 1929 p173

11 Op Cit Nov 1929 p175

12 Op Cit Mar 1930

converted it to a school for boys by adding a Victorian wing for classrooms and dormitories. The school became famous for its teaching methods and attracted pupils from across the world. Rowland Hill, (later Sir Rowland) and his brothers shared the headship. Rowland left teaching to work for the Post Office and introduced a number of reforms, of which the Penny Post system, with the Penny Black postage stamp, is the most well-known. When the school closed, in 1891, Tottenham Urban District Council bought the land. A year later, they opened the grounds as the first public park in Tottenham. In 1906, the building became the first museum in Tottenham, under the stewardship of the librarian, Mr F. J. West.

Archie had walked past the grounds every morning on his way to Risley Avenue School, and no doubt played in the park. He was very interested in the progress of work under way to refit the museum, as reports on the decorating and fitting of electric light and heating in the selected rooms circulated among the staff. An experienced junior assistant, Mr Rock, was appointed as Assistant Curator of the museum, not only to classify and label specimens, but also to give talks to classes of schoolchildren, who were encouraged to visit the museum[13].

The original order of the council on the regulation of the museum was reissued with minor revisions. In particular this stated:

No disorderly, intoxicated, or otherwise objectionable person shall be permitted in any part of the museum, nor shall persons be allowed to strike matches, smoke, carry naked lights, partake of refreshments, or bring dogs or other animals within the museum.

Other regulations stipulated opening times, protection of exhibits, and the use of the suggestions book. The re-established museum was officially opened by the Chairman of the Council and the Libraries and Museum Committee, Mr W. R Jackson, on Saturday 26th March 1927.[14]

During 1927, the Union of Postal Workers approached the Libraries and Museum Committee with a view to having the Morten Post Office Collection housed and displayed at the Bruce Castle Museum. W. V. Morten had been a telephone and Post Office worker and, by the time of his death in 1923, had built up a large collection of items of postal history. The UPW had purchased these and, as there was no national postal museum at the time, agreed that the former home of Sir Rowland Hill was an appropriate place to house the collection. Within the castle an exchange of rooms with the

---

13 Op Cit Jan 1927
14 Op Cit Mar 1927

Maternity and Child Welfare Committee had to be negotiated. As these were rented from the Education Committee, more discussions were required. All was eventually resolved; the collection safely housed, catalogued and labelled, and formally handed over by the Union for an official opening on 25th October 1928[15].

The refurbished museum also offered the opportunity for an improved service to schools. The provision of books for schools had been in place from 1921, but the museum offered a more immediate and visual experience. In the first six months after the refurbishment, many schools visited the museum. Classes in geology, history and economic products were held.[16] After a full year, the museum had welcomed one hundred and fifteen classes from twenty-four different schools and its value was fully recognised.[17] In addition, lantern lectures on the history of Old Tottenham were held in the museum and in the town hall, and were well supported by the local population.[18] On the strength of this, further series were arranged.

The opening of branch libraries, and the increase in borrowers, led to an increase in requests for the temporary interchange of books between the central and branch libraries. Although Archie was in charge of the central reference section, and thus not directly involved in issuing books on loan, there were inevitably requests for access to reference books held in the central library. The librarian pointed out to the committee that any book at any branch could be obtained on request. A telephone installed in each library enabled an enquiry to be given immediate attention. To go further would involve burdensome difficulties that would render the actual interchange unmanageable. He listed re-stocking, re-labelling, re-cataloguing and re-numbering as creating a great deal of extra work, which could not be undertaken at the time. The subject and author card catalogues at each library would also need overhauling. He indicated that it was the intention to create' over time, a card catalogue of total stock for each library, in addition to its own catalogue.[19]

By the end of 1929, the interchange service had been developed and was greatly appreciated by borrowers. The distribution of such books took up a great deal of staff time. In view of this, the librarian asked the committee to agree to an offer, from Wastell's Education Supply Service, in the High Road, to take on this work, with the use of a motorcycle and combination,

---

15 Op Cit Nov 1928
16 Op Cit Nov 1927
17 Op Cit May 1928
18 Op Cit Jan 1929
19 Op Cit June 1927 p129

for a three-month trial period at a fee of 4s 6d a week.[20]

Archie took a close interest in these issues as he was keen to pursue his career as a qualified professional. His father was the chief engineer of The London Public Omnibus Company when it was merged into the London General Omnibus Company and, as a result of the merger, he was made redundant at Christmas 1929. In spite of tireless efforts and impressive references, he was unable to obtain another position. After a short time the family had to move to a smaller, cheaper property in Rosebery Avenue. This period was very difficult for the family and put pressure on Archie, who was also courting his future wife, Phyllis Howard. These family and social pressures added to his frustration at the delays in resolving the potential promotions at Tottenham, and strengthened his determination to apply elsewhere for advancement.

When it became clear that the appointments at Tottenham would go through, Harry Fellows withdrew his application to Poplar. This strengthened Archie's chances as Fellows was the more experienced of the two. Archie was determined to try for the post and attended for interview.

---

20 Op Cit Dec 1929 p176

Chapter Three

Poplar 1930-36

"Sometimes it would appear as if it was a case of Poplar contra Mundum but the people do not mind." Borough calendar, 1926.

There was the need for a Senior Library Assistant in the Metropolitan Borough of Poplar at a starting salary of £200 per annum, rising by ten pounds a year to a maximum of £270. The duties would include detailed supervision of junior assistants; indexing, accessioning and cataloguing of new stock; counter duties; and the enticing prospect of suggesting additional stock. The successful applicant could also be in charge for up to a third of the day in the absence of the sub-librarian.[21] Archie knew that Poplar was an area of docklands, impoverished by the slump. It did not seem an attractive proposition at first sight, but he was young, idealistic and determined. He put in his application and did his best to research the area in detail.

The Official Guide to the borough for 1927[22] described four branch libraries. The new Senior Assistant would be required to help with preliminary work for two new branches being planned. The Poplar Branch was being prepared for open access during 1927, according to the guide. That would have been in operation by the time Archie applied. Archie was familiar with the system and enthusiastic about it. From the guide, it appeared that borrowing, reference rooms and reading rooms were all well used. Another feature Archie was pleased to see was the way the library worked together with the Education Committee of the London County Council and a committee of local teachers. A library staff member would give a lecture to every pupil in an elementary school, before they left at the age of 14, explaining what the public libraries had to offer and how to make best use of them. Classes from these schools came to hour-long, special study sessions on a wide range of subjects. There had been more than a hundred such visits in 1926. Parcels of books from the Juvenile Lending Department were also on loan to outlying schools. The libraries in the borough seemed increasingly popular as both membership and borrowings were growing.

In other ways, according to the guide, the Borough Council was improving conditions in the borough. Asphalt roads had been laid and mechanical

---

21 L/PMB/A/7/4 1916-1930 Minutes of Library Committee of MB Poplar.
22 Official Guide to the Metropolitan Borough of Poplar 1927.

sweepers introduced to clean up the area. It appeared that the Corporation's refuse destructor was of great interest to local authorities from around the country. Wash houses and public slipper baths had been provided, for those without bathroom facilities, and electricity was being generated for an increasing proportion of public lighting. Archie was also pleased to note that the infant death rate had fallen from 91% in the immediate aftermath of the Great War to a more recent 67%. All in all, he thought it seemed a worthwhile council to work for and he was delighted to receive an invitation to interview.

Three candidates had been selected for interview on the evening of 20th January 1930. With Harry Fellows withdrawing his application, Archie felt he had a real chance of success. He prepared for the interview with even more determination. One of the panel asked Archie about problems with the open access system.

"The system has been in operation in Tottenham since 1913, so the borrowers are accustomed to it," he replied.

"Do you have any problem with books glanced at and put back in the wrong place?" asked the librarian.

"Very little; borrowers are used to the system. When a new part of the service adopted the system, a junior assistant was never far away and encouraged people to replace books correctly. After a time it wasn't necessary."

"That is encouraging, at least," said the librarian.

Archie's only other challenger was Michael Pummell from Fulham. Mr Pummell had become a boy assistant directly from elementary school and so had five years more experience than Archie. The committee decided to appoint Mr Pummell, but the librarian, Harry Rowlatt, had been impressed by Archie.

"I liked your enthusiasm," he said, "and your answers on the open access system were sensible and practical. You've obviously taken the trouble to research the borough as well. I am sorry we couldn't appoint you, but we may have another post soon as the two new branches will be opening in the next few months." At the March library committee meeting the librarian pressed home his case[23]. McClellan was a good candidate; an earnest young man with four certificates, good Cambridge Junior and Senior Certificates and a determination to complete the Library Association qualification, with his bibliography examination, towards which he was studying at the time.

---

23 Borough of Poplar Library Committee mins. March 1930 p473

Tottenham had been a pioneer in the open access system and so he was familiar with its workings. In view of his suitability, Mr Rowlatt suggested and the committee agreed that, as a second Senior Assistant would be required for the new library in Fairfoot Road before October that year, and as they usually appointed an untrained assistant as holiday relief for four months, it would be beneficial to appoint Archie from June 1st [24] and dispense with the temporary post for the current year.

At the next meeting the chairman reported that he had withdrawn the recommendation because at the full Council meeting Councillor Easteal had objected. "In my opinion such an appointment is premature," he had said. "I am sure the holiday relief work can be carried out satisfactorily by an unqualified person. I happen to know that the man who provided temporary relief in 1929 is at present disengaged, and anxious to get the job."

"Circumstances are different this year," the chairman had replied. "The new library at Fairfoot Road requires a great deal of preliminary work in organisation and preparation. The work is of a technical character and will have to be carried out through the summer months in addition to the usual routine work. A qualified man will be much more use than an untrained one. The committee is anticipating the appointment by only a few months and the excess in costs would be slight." After further discussion, it was agreed to recommend the appointment of Mr McClellan on the previously agreed terms.

Archie was delighted to receive his letter of appointment, after having given up hope that Mr Rowlatt's remarks had been more than kindly consolation. He obtained a driving licence in May and bought a second-hand Baby Austin. He took up his appointment on 1st June. As he did so, he learned that his fellow candidate for the original vacancy, Michael Pummell, had died on 18th May, less than three weeks after commencing work, and that the post was being re-advertised.

An issue of immediate concern, that he had to ensure he could manage safely, was dealing with books returned by borrowers who had experienced smallpox in the household during the period of loan. These books were no longer destroyed, but the disinfection process had to be rigorous. Such books were to be thoroughly disinfected by the Public Health Department before being returned to the Poplar Library where they would be sealed in the formalin disinfecting box for a further period of one month. One of the boy assistants, whose family had suffered from the disease, had been

---

24 Op Cit

suspended on full pay for three weeks, on the advice of the Medical Officer, but was now safely back at work.[25]

At home, Archie enjoyed tinkering with his car and taking Phyllis Howard out for short runs. He continued attending the Quaker meetings but was becoming increasingly impressed by the way government was developing in the Soviet Union. It seemed, at the start of the 1930s, to offer a way forward from the economic depression and for world peace. Nearer to home, he was fascinated by the development of the huge airships the R100 and R101. These were planned to fly regularly across the Atlantic and to India. In the early autumn of 1930, four months after his move to Poplar, he was very excited by newspaper reports of final trial flights of the R101.

"It looks like they've finally got the R101 fit for its India trip. I'm going to fly to America in that, one day." said Archie. "It's in the paper today, Jack; look at this." He showed his brother a picture of the great airship being walked out of the hangar.

"Wow, how big is that?" said fifteen-year-old Jack. "It looks huge."

"It's twice as big as the German one from the war, the Graf Zeppelin. It's over two hundred and fifty yards long. It's doing a trial flight today. Look out for it tonight when you get home from school."

Archie was thrilled to see the R101 flying over Poplar. The newspapers reported that the trials had gone well, and the maiden flight to India was sent off with great excitement on the evening of Saturday 4th October 1930. On Sunday morning Archie listened for news on the wireless.

"We are interrupting our programme to bring you news of a major disaster. The R101, on its maiden flight, has crashed near Beauvais in France. It has been destroyed in a blazing inferno. No more than eight people are thought to have survived. The French emergency services are present at the scene."

Archie was horrified. "Have you heard the news, Dad? The R101 has crashed somewhere in France. Hardly anyone survived."

"Terrible," said his father. "I never trusted those things. All that gas was bound to blow up if there was a problem. A great balloon that size – much too difficult to control, especially in a strong wind. Tragic though."

Archie continued to follow the story in the newspapers and cut out pictures of the lying in state of the coffins and the Royal Navy Frigate that returned them for burial. He stuck the pictures in his photograph album along with his family photos. Archie read all the newspaper accounts in the

---

25 Op Cit 18th Feb 1930 p471

reference room at work during the following week. The general opinion was that the disaster would mark the end of British attempts to develop airships as a major means of air travel. I'll never get to fly in one now, he thought.

Meanwhile, progress on building the Fairfoot Road Branch and another in Wick Lane was good. Three boy assistants currently on probation were placed on the staff, and Archie helped in training them towards Library Association qualifications. The following month, the librarian was given permission to purchase two desks or writing tables (preferably second-hand), a typewriter (rebuilt, not more than £12.10s) and a clock for the new branches. Local pictures were to be framed for exhibition and a telephone line, shared with the public baths, put in at Wick Lane. This branch was opened without ceremony on 1st January 1931. An opening ceremony for the Fairfoot Lane Branch was scheduled for 7th March.[26]

Not all library users were positive in the way they used the facilities. One morning, a boy assistant came up to Archie at the desk.

"They're at it again, Mr Mac. They won't take any notice of me; told me to clear off. I don't know what to do, Mr Mac. No one else can get at the papers and they leave them in a right mess."

"You did the right thing, lad. I'll go through and have a word. Keep an eye on the desk for me," said Archie. In the reading room, three men had the sports pages spread across the tables. Other readers had already left. The men were comparing tips on the day's runners and marking up the names. They were arguing, good naturedly but in loud voices.

"Excuse me, gentlemen, but you are causing a disturbance and preventing other readers from using the facilities. I must ask you to return the newspapers to the racks and leave the reading room." Archie stood by the door.

"We ain't doin' no 'arm." Said one man, still wearing his cap. "'Ain't no jobs. We gotta make some cash somehow; families starvin' out there."

"Well, I am sorry but you can't use the library like this. It isn't fair to other users." Archie stood by as they filed out. Later that day, he reported the incident to the sub-librarian and the matter was taken up at Library Committee. It was clear that the other branches were experiencing similar problems. As a result, the librarian was instructed to obliterate the betting news from half of the daily newspapers[27].

Archie continued to study for the Bibliography Certificate to add to his

26 Op Cit pages 8,11, 17. Oct, Nov & Dec 1930 mins.
27 Op Cit Mins Jan 1931 pp22-3

Library Association qualifications. He obtained it in December 1930 and was congratulated by the library committee at the following February meeting. At the same meeting, *The Daily Worker* and *The Free Thinker* were added to the approved list of periodicals for the new branch at Fairfoot Road[28]. The branch was officially opened by the Mayor on Saturday 9th March 1931 and Archie spent the next two years as Senior Assistant librarian in charge.

Archie was now courting Phyllis Howard seriously. She was shy with boys, but loved a trip 'up the other end', as she referred to the West End, for a night at the dance hall or the theatre. Her father had just died and she was one of three sisters still living at home with her mother. Her mother's family had been nonconformist church goers and strong supporters of the Temperance Movement. Archie himself continued to hold strong anti-war ideals. Phyllis worked in the fur trade. Several boys had made it clear they would like to take her out but Archie was serious and ambitious, yet had a sense of fun which made her laugh. They grew close and, in March 1933, they married in the Methodist Church and moved into a small flat in Belmont Road in Tottenham[29].

Meanwhile, the pressure on sub-librarians and senior assistants had increased to such an extent that the Municipal Officers Association revived its campaign for proper recognition of the increased responsibilities by promoting Senior Assistants to grade C when they reached the highest scale point. Archie McClellan was mentioned as one of four who should be promoted. A detailed account of their responsibilities was provided by the borough librarian, and it was pointed out that, although the borough libraries occupied the second position in London, salaries compared unfavourably with other Metropolitan boroughs.[30] Discussion was deferred until the meeting the following month and it was subsequently decided that no action would be taken. In March 1934 one senior assistant had left and, after a further delegation from the Municipal Officers Association had been received by the library committee, it was agreed that two of the three would be promoted to grade C. Archie would not be so promoted as he was not yet at the top of grade B[31].

---

28 Op cit Mins Feb 1931 p27

29 Electoral Roll , West Green Ward Polling District H. 1933

30 Op Cit Mins14 Mar 1933, pp140-143

31 Op Cit Mins 17 Apr 1934

Chapter Four

The Young Librarian: Penge

"There has been an undoubted increase in the activities of the Library and a growth in its popularity."[32]

The librarian of the urban district of Penge, Mr S. J. Clarke, applied for retirement from April 5th 1936. The Public Library Committee exercised its powers to retain his services, from his desired date of departure until May 31, to enable the recruitment of a suitable replacement[33]. In the meantime, they revised and updated the listed duties of the librarian previously agreed in 1921. To comply with current practice, a few minor changes were made but one very significant duty was added, namely that the librarian *'shall reside at the Public Library premises.'* [34]

After their marriage in 1933, Arch and Phyl lived in the flat in Belmont Road in the West Green District of Tottenham. Phyllis gave up her job in the fur trade, and Archie continued to travel to Poplar to work. Archie came home one evening in the February of 1936, brimming with excitement. He showed Phyllis an advert for the post in Penge at £250 per annum, rising to £350 subject to satisfactory service. In particular, he pointed to the requirement to live on the premises.

"Let's go over and take a look at the weekend," he suggested. "It sounds just what we want."

"It would be good to get out of this little flat. How far is it from Tottenham?"

"It's not far away, still on the outskirts of London. It's a really nice area, and the job sounds ideal: a library to run in my own way. All the things I want to do. It would be wonderful."

When they saw the building at Oak Lawn, in Anerley Road, they were thrilled. Phyl was nervous of what, to her, was its grandeur after the poky little flat they were renting in Belmont Road, but she was not going to oppose the idea. The following month Archie came home to a letter inviting him, as one of six shortlisted candidates, to attend for interview on Monday April 6th, 1936 at 6.30 p.m.

Phyllis sat at home as 6.30 approached and drank a cup of tea. She hoped he had managed to get there in time. How long would it take from Poplar?

32 Urban District Council of Penge. Minutes of proceedings for the years 1937 – 38 Annual Report of the Public Library Committee., p37
33 Urban District Council of Penge. Minutes of proceedings for the years 1935-6 p308 27 Jan 1936
34 Op Cit p312 Clause 18

Had he left enough time? Good job I made him put on a clean shirt this morning, she thought, I just hope his collar hasn't got too creased. I should have given him a spare one so he could change it before he went in to the interview. Please, Archie, don't mention politics, she begged. If they start at 6.30 and there are six of them, however long will it take? Will they tell them tonight? She wound up the gramophone and put on *Sally* by Gracie Fields.

Phyl sat back and let that voice she loved so much absorb her. By eight o'clock she began to worry again. She remembered her knitting. A cardigan for the cool evenings in spring and autumn; would it be fashionable enough for Penge? They're so much posher there. She put the National Radio on, but the news was all about Stalin and Hitler: She turned it off; she had enough to worry about. Please don't mention politics, Archie, she said it out loud this time; they aren't the same in Penge as they are in Poplar. She looked at the clock again, quarter to eleven, surely they must have decided by now.

She heard a key in the lock. "Well?" she said. "How did it go? Did you get it?" He looks absolutely washed out, she thought.

"They will let us know," he said. "Is there any tea?" She made a fresh pot as he described the interview. "It seemed to go well, but the other candidates were good. Well, most of them anyway." Two days later a letter with the Urban District Council of Penge monogram arrived. He brought it to the table.

"This is it," he said, reaching for his paper knife.

"Well? What does it say? Have you got it?" As he read the letter, his face broke into a broad smile.

"I have been offered the post, on condition I pass a medical examination," he said.

"Oh well done, Archie." She slid her arms round his neck and they hugged each other. The medical proved to be the formality he had anticipated and, to his great delight, he was appointed with effect from June 1st 1936.

Phyllis soon overcame her nervousness as they moved into the more spacious accommodation above the library at Oak Lawn. Archie could work much more conveniently without having to travel, and Phyllis herself would spend many evenings, after the library was closed, sitting cross-legged on the floor in front of the shelves, reading from the wide range of fiction available. They also had an annual holiday entitlement of twenty-four working days. They could now afford a better car and so, over the following few years, they explored the country from Devon and Cornwall up to Scarborough and Robin Hood's Bay. Phyllis felt this was the best time of their lives. They were young, had no ties and enough money to enjoy their lives and anticipate a happy and prosperous future.

The living quarters at Oak Lawn included a tower rising a further two storeys above the rest of the building. The tower contained the bathroom and, reputedly, a ghost. The views from the tower were spectacular. The Crystal Palace stood in its extensive gardens. The great curve of the glass roof could be seen at the crest of Streatham Hill as Anerley Road curved round towards the entrance. Arch and Phyl would walk up the road and stroll through the gardens. In late summer they would wander up the Grand Central Walk, pausing to admire the great fountains on either side. Facing them at the top of the rise stood the magnificent frontage of glass and metal; such a contrast to Belmont Road and Lordship Lane.

On a Monday night at the end of November in their first year there, Archie came out of his office a few minutes after eight in the evening. Phyl was sitting cross-legged on the floor reading *Emma* by Jane Austen.

"Let's go up for a cup of tea," said Archie. "I've finished for today. Bring your book with you. We can always pop it back in the morning."

Phyl stood up, still reading, and walked towards him. He slid an arm round her shoulder and kissed her forehead. She smiled up at him and closed the book.

"Just put the kettle on, love, I need to pop to the bathroom; I'll be there in a moment," said Archie at the top of the stairs. A moment later he shouted to her, "Phyl come and look." She heard the urgency in his voice and feared he'd hurt himself. She ran through towards the bathroom. He was standing by the window staring out.

"What is it?" she said.

"Look at that. It's on fire. The Crystal Palace is on fire." As they looked, the blaze raged higher; smoke and debris was blowing back over the gardens in the strong November wind.

"The sky's bright red above it," said Phyl. "And the smoke… great red clouds of it. It's terrifying."

"It looks like that glass dome has fallen in, you know, from the middle of the roof." said Archie.

They could hear the bells of fire engines roaring up the Anerley Road. Police cars too, were speeding through the traffic as crowds began to gather.

They stood watching for an hour, unable to tear themselves away from the devastating scene.

"Let's have that cup of tea," said Archie. "We can look again before we go to bed." Once they were sitting in the lounge, the enormity of the catastrophe began to sink in. "John Logie Baird was experimenting with television in the South Tower. If that goes up in flames, it will take him years to make up for it. I was hoping I might be able to build one myself in a few years' time. You know, like that crystal set wireless."

"Oh Archie, what do you want with that fancy stuff? You've got your wireless; a proper one I mean. Let's see if this is on there yet."

"I'm going to have another look," said Archie, going back to the tower. There was a muffled bang. "Did you hear that? They've blown something up near the South Tower. I hope Logie Baird's experiment isn't damaged."

The National Radio was bringing news that crowds of people were arriving to witness the destruction. Winston Churchill was reported to be visiting. "It's the end of an era," he was quoted as saying. In the weeks that followed, the newspapers were full of stories and interviews, but the site was sealed off and left derelict. Only the two towers remained and although in the springtime Archie and Phyl still strolled up to the gardens, they found the sealed-off ruin a depressing backdrop to their walks.

The library Archie took over had many positive features. In particular, it had a strong junior department to which the education committee contributed funds. Local schools valued highly the consignments of books, sent from the Junior Department every month, for use in class. A series of well-attended lectures and film displays on a variety of subjects was given for children in the winter months. The lectures were delivered by a group of volunteers ably assisted over many years by a Mr H. W. Shepherd, as lanternist.[35] There was a suggestion book, in which borrowers could record books they would like the library to add, and many of these suggestions were taken up. The more advanced students benefited from the affiliation with the National Central Library. This enabled students to access books of a specialist nature which had no place in a general lending library.[36]

Other pleasing features in place on Archie's arrival were the binding facilities, the display of holiday literature in the lending department and an annual auction of newspapers and periodicals. The 'Situation Vacant'

---

35 Urban District Council of Penge, Minutes of Proceedings 1936-37 pp35-6 27th April 1936. A lanternist operated an early form of slide projector using lantern slides.
36 Op Cit p38 27th April 1936.

pages of the daily papers were displayed in the porch from 7.00 a.m. This allowed people to study them under cover and take an early train into town in the hope of filling a vacancy. The local newspaper, the *Beckenham and Penge Advertiser*, was very helpful in publicising the various activities of the library and listing books added each month. Archie was supported in his duties by four female assistants.[37]

The annual report of the Public Library Committee for Mr Clarke's final year stated as part of a brief introduction, "such information as may be gleaned from the bald statement of statistics is here appended.[38]" The report lived up to this description but Archie was determined that, under his leadership, future reports would include far more explanation and interpretation. The following three years saw continuing increases in the library's activities and in its popularity.

In his first year in charge, Archie introduced a number of changes, the success of which foreshadowed the more comprehensive developments he put forward in his plans for Tottenham ten years later. He made it clear from the outset that he valued the local knowledge and expertise of the assistant librarians. He proposed regular meetings to discuss problems and solutions and asked them to approach him at any time with concerns or ideas. At first they were confused and suspicious of this young man of twenty-eight, and a little embarrassed to raise complaints or suggestions. They had been used to Mr Samuel Clarke who had been in the job for thirty-eight years and had finally retired at the age of sixty-five. Their main task had been to keep things running smoothly. They had not been expected to contribute ideas. Archie emphasised that the most important part of the library is the book stock. There needed to be enough books; they should be in a good clean condition, representative in scope and responsive to the needs of users.

"On that last point, Mr McClellan, we find the suggestion book very helpful and we have usually been able to obtain most of the requests," said Miss Goodchild, the second assistant.

"The trouble is, though, that people often ask us about books they'd like, but if we ask them to enter the details in the suggestion book they say it doesn't matter," said Miss Cole, the first assistant. "And of course they don't always know all the details."

"Do you get many such comments?"

---

37 Op Cit pp39-41
38 Op Cit p34

"Yes," said Miss Cole and the others nodded their agreement.

"It happens all the time," said Miss Goodchild.

"I'll think about that and see what we can do. If we could take on board their requests, it would help us convince them of our commitment to a book stock responsive to their needs. This brings me to the main task I feel should be our focus this year: a complete revision of the book stock." He paused to gauge their reaction. They looked at each other nervously. "It will be demanding, but we will be able to offer a much better service as a result. It will clearly take time but we can approach it methodically, starting with the least used areas first."

"That dusty old corner where nobody even bothers to look any more," said Miss Goodchild.

"That's where we will start, then," said Archie.

During the next year, the complete book stock was overhauled. Over seven thousand books were discarded as obsolete, of these some six hundred were replaced by more attractive editions as still having something of value, and over two thousand new books were added. The result was a threefold increase in borrowing as each section was completed. The loans continued to increase when the revision was finished. In particular, a greater proportion of non-fiction books were borrowed. This was due in part to the more attractive editions and in part to the increase in up-to-date stock. In addition, a special display bookcase was introduced, providing some very attractive displays on a series of non-fiction topics.

Once he had seen the enthusiasm of the assistants as the loans increased and compliments about the displays brought greater job satisfaction, Archie suggested that, as often as circumstances allowed, they should note down the requests and comments of borrowers, including name and address, so that individual needs could better be met and borrowers should have a sense that their interests were being followed up. Detailed assistance was always on hand for serious readers and specialised booklists were provided and revised at regular intervals. The increased demand led to the issue of a second non-fiction ticket on request and a complete revamp of the system for dealing with overdue books. Both these innovations led to a significant increase in loans.

The increase in usage continued throughout Archie's time at Penge. He introduced a quarterly bulletin, "Book News" which sold at 2d a copy. Its list of new books added contributed to the big rise in interest in non-fiction sections. Also popular was "The New Book Information Service". Readers completed a form about their special interests and were informed when new books on the subject were added[39].

In the Reading Room, Archie's only immediate change was the introduction of a table reserved for women readers. This proved very popular. In the following year the magazines were put into new transparent covers for periodicals, which were more attractive and more hygienic. The reference section needed a major overhaul. All the books were classified and arranged in numerical order on the shelves and many new books added. Pamphlets were organised in the same way and a special Motorists' Reference Library was set up to hold a whole range of instruction books from vehicle manufacturers. No doubt Archie made full use of this facility for his own car maintenance.

To further encourage serious researchers and students, a quiet area was set aside with tables, scrap paper and writing facilities provided. A sustained 25% increase in its use followed. Archie was determined that the reference library should become a centre for commercial and general information in the district. The library staff made good use of the section in answering enquiries from the reference books.

It was clear to Archie that a habit of reading should develop in childhood, as children formed the foundation of the future borrowing public. This was welcome news to the local head teachers and the Education Officer, who were delighted to strengthen further their links with the library service. The annual grant continued throughout Archie's time as librarian and contributed to the continuing provision of the small book collections sent to schools every month.

Within the library itself, Archie introduced major changes. The furniture in the Junior Library was more appropriately arranged and the room was brightened by redecoration, with popular characters from children's fiction illustrated on the walls. Coloured discs on the backs of books provided a simplified classification system. Books for girls were differentiated from those for boys and the children learned to replace books correctly. Archie gave lectures to school leavers on the benefits of the Public Library in life after school, and a library assistant ran story hours for children aged 7 – 9. In the winter months, the lectures for children given by a wide range of lecturers continued to attract good audiences. In addition, film shows and musical evenings were arranged in the town hall. Another popular event at the town hall was the Annual Book Exhibition and the essay competition

---

39 Urban District Council of Penge,. Minutes of proceedings for the year 1938-39 25th April 1938, p36

held in connection with this[40].

In his three years at Penge, Archie transformed the Public Library Service, but he could not have achieved this without close attention to the detail of day-to-day management, as well as the broad vision of what the service should offer. He engaged his four library assistants in enthusiastic support for the extra work involved in implementing the changes and in adjusting their own roles in the service. He found ways to save on day-to-day costs to which the staff gave their full support. Publicity through special displays on topical issues such as motoring, gardening and international affairs drew a wide range of people who read the details in the *Beckenham and Penge Recorder*. Such was the impact of his time at Penge that the library committee were able to state to the full council in May 1939,

The Committee is delighted to note the increasing popularity of the Library Services for no better criterion of its efficiency and place in the life of the people of Penge is possible, and places on record its high appreciation of the work of the librarian and his assistants.[41]

As well as the longer holidays exploring the West Country and the North East in the open-top Austin and camping or staying in bed and breakfast accommodation, they had day and weekend trips with their families. Archie got on well with his in-laws. Many of Phyl's brothers and brothers–in-law were closer to Archie in age than his own brothers. They enjoyed days out at Clacton or Jaywick Sands, picnicking, swimming and relaxing on the beach. They visited Archie's parents and his little sister, Joyce, in Rosebery Avenue and Phyl's mother and her sister Pauline in Baronet Grove, the house where Phyl had grown up.

The shadow of 'the gathering storm' of the war to come lay over the happiness of these few years of young married life and increasing prosperity. Archie took a keen interest in the fate of communist and socialist regimes in the Soviet Union and Spain. His pacifist leanings led him to share the brief optimism of Neville Chamberlain's negotiated compromise with Hitler. Local authorities were discussing arrangements for air raid wardens and the precautions that would be needed in the event of war. The Nazi-Soviet pact and the 'Pact of Steel' between Hitler and Mussolini destroyed what optimism there had been. The success of General Franco in the Spanish Civil War and the further aggression of Russia, Italy and Japan brought the prospect of war frighteningly close. Phyllis was terrified, not only of the

40 Op cit pp39-40
41 Urban District Council of Penge,. Minutes of proceedings for the year 1939-40 22nd May 1939 p.74

dangers of invasion, but of Archie being arrested for his political views and connections.

Archie himself was deeply disillusioned by the Russian pact with Hitler, and by its invasion of Finland. He detested Fascism and all it represented and told Phyl he would not hesitate to serve in the fight against it. She didn't know if this made her more or less frightened of the future. In the meantime, Archie felt that Penge and Beckenham were particularly vulnerable to bombing should the war start, and that he had achieved most of what he could at the library. He had modernised all the areas of library activity and increased its use and popularity and was anxious to develop his ideas on a broader scale.

"I think we should move out of London," he said.

"But why? Where to? I've never lived out of London. The family are all here. You've got a good job. We've got a good life here," said Phyl.

"There's going to be a war. London will be the main target. I want to keep you as safe as possible, especially if I'm called up."

"But where would we go?"

"There's a librarian's job going in Chelmsford. I thought I'd apply for that."

"That's miles away. Why there?"

"I've done all I can at this library. I want a new challenge. It's a bigger library; it serves a bigger area, and it's out of London. Anyway, Madge and Will live in Hutton, which is only a few miles away, and Lil and Sid are at Hatfield Peverel, which is only a few miles the other way and you're used to visiting them, so it won't all be strange."

Young Archie

Risley Avenue Central School
Archie is second from left in front row

No More War demonstration, 1922.
Young Archie stands in the front with his hands together

Archie Gets Married

Archie McClellan

Phyllis Howard

Archie's Parents

Poplar in the 1930's

R101 over Poplar October 1930

Opening of Fairfoot Road
Library.

Reading Room in the Docklands Settlement on
Isle of Dogs, Poplar, 1930s

Penge Pictures

Oak Lawn, The Penge Public Library

On Holiday, Robin Hood Bay

Contemplating the move to Penge

Flying Officer McClellan

AIR TRAINING CORPS
No. 276 Chelmsford Squadron
JULY, 1945

Third Row, seated, Fourth from left—W/O Thomson; F/O's A. W. McCellan, M. Innis; F/Lt. G. F. Purvis (C.O.); His Worship the Mayor of Chelmsford (Councillor S. C. Taylor), Chairman of the Committee; F/O S. Edgar (Adj); F/O W. Clough; W/O W. Hicks (Bandmaster).

Cartoon by one of the cadets when Mac returned from Grange-over-Sands course

Chelmsford: The end of the war

Chelmsford Emergency Centre

The Jowett 1947

3 The Drive,
Hatfield Peverel

Three Wolf Cub Sixers
Keith McClellan on right

Chapter Five

Chelmsford

War on the Home Front

Phyllis was listening to the wireless. The news from Europe seemed more threatening every day. Archie seemed resigned to the inevitability of war. All his optimism and faith in the socialist and communist peace ideals had been destroyed by Stalin's pact with Hitler and Franco's victory in Spain. Was that a car she heard coming into the drive? She went to the window. He was just getting out of the Austin. Was there a bounce in his step?

"We're moving to Chelmsford," he said, hurrying towards her with a broad grin and his arms stretched wide. She stepped into his embrace and received a smacking kiss on each cheek.

"Oh Arch, well done. I knew you were bound to get it."

"There were ten of us there but the decision was unanimous. I start on September 1st."

"But it's the middle of July already. How are we going to get everything sorted out by then?"

Phyllis felt torn between pride in his achievement and fear of moving so far out of town. Where would they live? There was no home attached to the library as there was in Penge. And the war…. supposing he was called up and she was left on her own, miles from family and friends, knowing no one, terrified he'd be killed. The last three years had been wonderful; the sort of life she'd always dreamed of. They were comfortably off, had lovely holidays and no worries about rent or housing. She'd really got to feel at home in Penge. Now all that was going to change.

"I'll get £300 a year with an extra twenty for each of the next three years if I do well, which I will," said Archie. "Any chance of a cup of tea?"

Phyllis felt a twinge of guilt. She should have brewed it by now.

"Sorry, love," she said. He followed her to the kitchen.

"The chairman told me they were really impressed. Said they'd had seventy applications altogether but had called the ten most impressive ones. But I stood out, he said, and they were looking forward to me starting. It's a very good library, much bigger than this one and there's a very nice museum there too. It's run by the same committee but has its own curator." His enthusiasm softened her nervousness, as she made the tea and took two cups and saucers from the cupboard.

Archie submitted his resignation to the Library Committee at Penge to date from August 31st. Phyl had been checking the *Essex Chronicle* and the other local papers for possible places to live.

"Arch," she said," you wouldn't believe this, but there's a bungalow to rent only two doors up from Madge and Will in Hutton. That's not too far from Chelmsford, is it?" Madge was her sister. She was married to Will Simmons, who worked in the fur trade and bred budgerigars in an aviary in his garden. They had a little boy called David.

Archie pulled out the road atlas they used on holidays. "Quite a short drive; only about twelve miles. We could drive over and have a look at the weekend."

Madge and Will were delighted. "You can babysit David for us, Phyl," smiled Madge.

They moved in at the end of the month and Phyl soon made the bungalow feel like a home. Archie took up his new appointment on the first day of September 1939 and two days later the nation was at war. Like families throughout the country, Arch and Phyl had sat silently by the radio as Neville Chamberlain made his fateful statement following the German invasion of Poland. The impact of the war was to dominate Archie's time at Chelmsford from the outset. Within a fortnight, the government announced the rationing of motor spirit, or petrol as we call it now. Archie took his registration book to the Post Office and picked up his coupons.

"I just hope there's enough to get to work every day," he said, "It's one coupon a gallon at the moment but there's no guarantee it'll stay that much."

"What will you do?" said Phyl.

"Well, we may have to move into Chelmsford." As the evenings shortened, the impact of the blackout increased. There was no street lighting and cars were restricted to shaded headlights and white painted bumpers. When winter set in, Archie found travelling to and from work more and more difficult.

"We'll have to move to Chelmsford," he said. "It's too dangerous to drive, I can never be sure of fuel, and they are stopping the bus services early now."

"I suppose we'll have to," said Phyl. "But I can't say I look forward to it. It's been good to be with Madge, on her own with little David. Always worrying about Will."

"This war is a dreadful business," said Archie. "We can only concentrate on essentials. I'll make some enquiries. We don't really have a choice, love."

A few weeks later they moved to an upstairs flat in Glebe Road in Chelmsford.

As a newcomer to the town and the authority, Archie was faced with an immediate staffing crisis. Two people had resigned and would have to be replaced, while holidays and illness had reduced numbers to the bare minimum needed to maintain a service. A food control centre had been set up in the reference library. A full reference service was maintained, although the room had to be closed at sunset for the whole of September to comply with blackout regulations. Meanwhile borrowing, particularly of non-fiction and children's books, increased and there was an increase in registrations of new borrowers. Interviewed by the *Essex Chronicle*, Archie said that, although borrowing had initially fallen, it was now back to normal and steadily increasing. People were looking for lighter reading to take their minds off the war. "There are signs that people do not want to read anything too serious, too technical or too involved. There is, for instance, no special demand even for books like Hitler's *Mein Kampf*" [42]

Archie asked the committee to allow the loan of more than one book of fiction and one of non-fiction, as borrowers from outlying districts would find it especially difficult to access the library frequently. This was agreed for the length of the emergency period only. Archie was able to meet with the chairman to present some readers' suggestions and agree on new and replacement books.

The days were already shortening as winter approached. Archie obtained estimates for the supply and fitting of blackout blinds and fittings to the ceiling lights so that the library could resume normal opening hours. The committee rejected the system as too expensive. They proposed that a simpler method of blinds fitted on wire guides be tried and evaluated [43].

At the same October meeting, Mrs Pain, who was acting curator to cover for her husband, brought the committee up to date on museum developments over the previous six months.   She reported that the museum had been closed for nine days to enable the staff to pack and remove irreplaceable objects to a safer place. In spite of this, visitor numbers continued to rise. The increase in local visitors was boosted by the growing number of evacuees. The extended school holidays had led to more visits and lectures. A number of teachers had attended to sketch natural history objects and to note descriptions of them. This would no doubt continue in the light of the

---

42 News Chronicle 29th Sept 1939
43 Minutes of Chelmsford Borough Public Library and Museum Committee, 9 Oct 1939 pp280-89

collection of big game heads among the donations. Newcomers to Essex had recorded their delight at the quality of such a museum, open to the public free of charge. In the light of these positive reports, the acting curator asked the committee to support the request from the Museum Association to make every effort to keep the museum open during the war. [44]

Archie took a keen interest in the Oaklands Museum, as he had at Bruce Castle in Tottenham. He familiarised himself with the layout, the most interesting exhibits and the services offered to the community. It became increasingly clear that the curator, Mr Pain, would not return after his leave of absence. At the committee meeting in February 1940, his contract was terminated and his wife was given two weeks' leave[45]. No provision for a curator's salary was made in the estimates for the new financial year. Mrs Pain was not retained. Thus Archie became *de facto* curator. He enjoyed the role and was conscientious in ensuring the service was maintained and developed. At the July meeting of the committee he pointed this out. He asked the committee to consider formalising the position. They agreed but voted to defer the consideration of remuneration until the October meeting[46].

The police had removed a small number of firearms likely to be of use to undesirable persons. They had been stored safely. Archie, as acting curator, had also removed all maps likely to be of use to the enemy.[47] Meanwhile, another issue raised at the committee meeting in February 1940 was the crisis that had developed in the Citizens Advice Bureau. It had reached a point where it was threatened with closure but a director had been appointed who was willing to take responsibility. She would report to Archie, who, as borough librarian, was nominally the controlling officer. Thus within six months of his appointment, Archie's responsibilities had already grown and would continue to do so throughout the war.

Meanwhile, Phyllis was feeling more and more cut off. She could no longer pop downstairs to borrow a book or have a quick read. Archie was at work for increasing hours of the day. Rationing of food and clothing had been introduced early in the year and the advance of the Germans through Belgium, Holland and France was terrifying. What made it worse, as spring turned to summer, was the inevitable progression of her pregnancy. They had never intended to have children. That's what they had agreed. But as the war became more threatening, Archie felt they should have a child. If he

---

44 Op Cit Acting Curator's Report.
45 Chelmsford Borough Library and Museum Report 29th Feb 1940 p289
46 Chelmsford Borough Library and Museum Report 8th July 1940 p293
47 Op Cit July 1940 p293

was called up and killed, as could so easily happen, she would at least have his child to remember him by. Phyl had been reluctant; the whole process made her nervous, but the thought of losing Archie was unbearable. At least a child would be a permanent gift from their few years of happiness together.

By the middle of summer, the Germans had driven the Expeditionary Force out of France and the French had surrendered. The evacuation at Dunkirk had shown patriotism and ingenuity. It was a proud moment, but the fact was Britain was losing. Hitler was even now preparing to invade. At its May meeting, the borough council agreed to the use of the children's department of the library as the Casualty Information Bureau for the area. Archie agreed to act as casualty officer and to organise volunteer helpers to run the bureau[48]. Borough council staff helped in preparing road blocks, especially for the A12. Pill boxes were built to protect the Hoffmann and Marconi factories.

The air raid siren sounded with monotonous regularity as the Battle of Britain was fought out overhead. Already bombs were dropping over London and the North, as well as the harbours and factories on the coast. It was all too terrifying. On August 19th, a line of bombs fell between Chelmer Road and Gainsborough Crescent, killing three people and injuring six more. Four houses were demolished and several others badly damaged. Further raids followed. On October 13th, the Mayor and his whole family were killed by a direct hit on their house in the London Road. By October the Battle of Britain seemed to have been won, delaying an invasion indefinitely, but the blitz on cities was continuing. The railway line to Liverpool Street and the A12 road to London guided the enemy planes over Chelmsford. With the baby due at any time, Phyllis lived in dread.

After the October meeting Archie seemed pleased.

"They've finally agreed to pay me for being museum curator. It's an extra thirty pounds a year and they're backdating it to July," he said.

"Not before time, what with the baby due in a week or two and all the rationing. That's if we don't get bombed out anyway."

"I'm sure we'll be all right. Mind you, they've let me put some protection up against the glass splinters if the library is hit in a raid. It is getting serious. Especially with all the extra book issues, and there are no end of visitors to the museum."[49]

48 Chelmsford at War 1939 – 45, Andrew J Begent, p4
49 Chelmsford Borough Library and Museum Committee Minutes Oct 14th 1940 p298

"It's about time they paid you for it then." said Phyl.

"Well, they are now. Cup of tea?"

Three weeks later, on 7th November, Archie was sitting at his wife's bedside in St John's Hospital. He held a tiny baby boy in his arms. He was wrapped in a white woollen shawl which covered all but his face and his tiny hands. Archie marvelled at the minute fingers and tried to rub noses with his day-old son who burst into a roar of protest.

"Don't Arch, he's too young yet. Just hold him tight and give him a kiss: a gentle one!" said Phyl.

They discussed names. Arch liked Keith because it sounded Scottish and went well with McClellan, and Phyl liked it because it couldn't be shortened. For his middle name they stuck to tradition and gave him Phyl's maiden name. He was registered as Keith Howard McClellan. Arch would not have him christened.

"He can make up his own mind when he's old enough," he said.

"Are you sure? Everyone has their baby christened," said Phyl uncertainly.

"That's no reason. He should be able to decide such things for himself."

The bombing raids continued throughout November and December 1940. The police headquarters buildings were seriously damaged and many houses destroyed. Archie was in great demand as casualties mounted and the Casualty Information Bureau volunteers were recruited, trained and pressed into action. Early in the new year an Air Training Corps was formed in the town. It was officially known as 278 Squadron and soon had well over a hundred and fifty boys wanting to enrol. Archie had a long standing interest in engines, perhaps inherited from his father's work on London's buses.

"They are looking for volunteer flying officers to train the lads in maintaining and servicing the aero engines. I've a good mind to apply," he said one evening.

"You already do too much," said Phyl. "What with the C.A.B. and the Casualty Bureau, quite apart from the library and museum."

"But this is something positive. It's like a hobby, and a big contribution to the war effort."

"I can see you are determined. I'll see even less of you than I do already, and your little boy won't recognise you. You're hardly ever here when he's awake," said Phyl.

Archie was commissioned as an acting flying officer for the duration of hostilities on 6th May 1941[50]. He was happy working with the engines, but most of all he enjoyed training the young men. He had had his first taste of teaching in his latter years at Tottenham, when he had helped new assistants with their Library Association qualifications. He continued to serve throughout the war until the scheme came to an end in October 1946. Three days after Archie's commission was awarded, a major bombing raid hit the Marconi works very near to his flat in Glebe Road. Two bombs hit the factory, killing seventeen night workers, and one bomb hit residential properties in Marconi Road. Flames from the factory spread to a flour mill in Townfield Street. Glebe Road linked these two streets and was lucky to escape serious damage. Two weeks later, flats in Coval Lane were hit. Six people were killed and eight more injured[51]. Ten flats were demolished and a large number of houses and shops were damaged. These bombs fell very close to the flat in Glebe Road and the bus station and library were damaged, as Archie found when he walked to work next morning.

"It's only a matter of time before we're hit. We've got no shelter to speak of," said Phyl. "I think we should move to somewhere safer."

"There is a plan for Morrison shelters. We should be eligible for one. I gather they are starting to issue them next month," said Archie.

"I think we should go and see Lil and Sid at Hatfield Peverel. See if they know of anywhere to rent around there."

"I suppose it's not far. At least there's quite a good bus service," said Archie.

***

At the library, the basement used as an air raid shelter provided an opportunity for what was described at the council meeting in December as 'unacceptable misbehaviour'. As a result the basement would be locked at night. The warden would open it when the air raid warning siren sounded. At the same meeting it was also reported that school children had been misbehaving in the reading room. Archie was instructed to write to head teachers asking them to emphasise the need for treating books with care. In the new year head teachers would be expected to issue permits to those who needed to use the room.[52]

Quarterly reports to the Library and Museum Committee continued to show that borrower requests for additions to the bookstock were considered

---

50 *The London Gazette* 11 July 1941 p4008
51 Begent p16.
52 Chelmsford Borough Library and Museum Minutes 1st Dec 1941 p321

and agreed, particularly if second-hand copies could be found. New books were added and worn or outdated copies withdrawn. Initially these were offered to the various military units in the locality, but later, when Archie was appointed the honorary librarian for Chelmsford Prison, their library was offered the withdrawn books first. Any they did not want were offered to the Y.M.C.A. and the remaining books, if any, were offered to the military units. The range of magazines and newspapers was reduced to save costs. An application from Hearst Advertising to forego payment of part of the fee for providing bookmarks with adverts to the reference library was rejected, and an application was made for a Ministry of Education grant towards funding the extra burden of providing for evacuees. Archie calculated that, on the basis of one pound per eight hundred refugees, they should be entitled to three pounds.[53]

---

53 Report to Chelmsford Borough Council Jan 1940 p275

Chapter Six

Hatfield Peverel

"Mr McClellan is indispensable at this time. A very serious situation will arise if deferment is not granted." Chelmsford Town Clerk.

Phyl's sister, Lillian, twelve years her senior, had been like a second mother to her as she grew up. She ran a grocery store in Hatfield Peverel and her husband, Sid, had a barber's shop next door. Both shops fronted their house and garden. Rationing was now biting hard so that supplies were often difficult to come by, but Lil usually managed to keep her customers up to their full rations. As the winter approached, Lil told Phyl that the old lady who owned the bakery, Mrs Cleave, had one of the semis on the main road to let; number three, The Drive. Arch and Phyl met Mrs Cleave, inspected the property and decided it was ideal. They moved there in January 1942.

The Drive was a short-weed-and-shingle surfaced track that left the A12 Harwich/London road to serve four semi-detached houses and Mrs Cleave's field. It ran behind a hawthorn hedge, parallel to the main road, before rejoining it through a gateway. Greying paint was peeling and curling away from the shrivelled, knotted gateposts at each end, their rusted hinges devoid of gates. In contrast, the houses were new and bright. Hollyhocks, leaning out over the shingle track, lined the front fence; rose bushes flanked the concrete path to the front door, and a small square lawn housed a concrete birdbath at its centre.

Inside the front door, a small hallway gave on to stairs and a passage through to the kitchen.In the living room, a walnut dining table stood against the wall with two chairs each side. On the opposite wall, the light brown tiled fireplace shared a chimney with the house next door. The window looked out onto a lawn, which lay in the shadow of the house. A large, asbestos-panelled shed stood to the left and the lawn opened out into sunlight beyond it. A flowerbed bordered by a trellis cut off the further, neglected length of garden where fruit trees flowered and fruited among the weeds. To ease the restrictions of rationing, Phyl would pick the plums and pears when they ripened. She would boil them and seal them into Kilner jars and store them in the walk-in larder under the stairs. To the right, a privet hedge and lilac tree almost blocked out the neighbours, although their rabbit hutches could be seen through small gaps in the privet.

The air raid warning siren a quarter of a mile away, at the local fire station, sounded several times a week, as German bombers followed the A12 for their night raids on London. Viewed from the Morrison shelter under the table, only the chance flash of a passing searchlight or stray incendiary relieved the darkness of the blackout. A tall walnut-veneered wireless stood on a spindle-legged occasional table in the alcove between the fireplace and the window. The curved dial indicated numbers and places beyond imagination, yet the pointer remained on the BBC Home Service unless reception was poor and delicate fine-tuning was required. Brown Bakelite knobs controlled volume and tuning and a smell of burning dust arose from the back of the set after an hour of 'Family Favourites' or 'Workers Playtime' and the one o'clock news.

On an end wall, the craggy seascape of the North-East coast formed the background for a longhaired youth, clothed in late nineteenth century style. Above the table, a black-and-white print of a man driving a horse and cart with a Lakeland fell rising behind him was labelled, in Archie's handwriting, 'Old Man of Coniston'. Both pictures were powerful reminders of the carefree holidays before the loss of the car at the outbreak of war.

The front room, with its bay window looking out over the front garden was used only on special occasions. Upstairs, Arch and Phyl had the front bedroom and put Keith, now a toddler, in the back room overlooking the back garden. There was a bathroom at the top of the stairs and a box room at the far end of the landing. Sometimes, an anti-aircraft gun, towed along the A12 in pursuit of the raiding aircraft, would be fired with an explosive noise. The nearest houses shuddered from the shock wave.

Phyl was not used to village life. Her sister Lil was her one consolation. Turning right from The Drive, Lil and Sid's shops were only two hundred yards or so along the pavement. The butcher was some way beyond. Meat was strictly rationed, except for offal such as hearts, liver and kidneys, but rabbit or chicken were available at a price. Beef, pork and mutton were very rare as they took up too many coupons. If she turned left from The Drive, she immediately passed Creswell's Drug Store and a little further on was the greengrocer's, run by Mrs Wood. The bakery, owned by Mrs Cleave but run by her son Aubrey, was a few yards further on. All the shopkeepers were friendly enough, but Phyl made no friends that she would invite round for a cup of tea and a chat. Lil was the only exception.

Further War Problems

Archie caught the bus into Chelmsford, from the bus stop opposite The Drive, every morning, except on the rare occasions when he had the use of the Ministry of Information car, a large black Austin with a double loudspeaker on the roof. Under the Ministry of Information, a number of campaigns were run to gain support for the war effort. Archie was the secretary of the local committee for the duration of the war. The library was involved in *Warship Week*, with programmes on sale in reception at sixpence a copy. For the summer months, a *Holidays at Home* scheme was organised in the area. At the height of the summer, the museum provided interesting afternoon events as part of the programme. Towards the end of 1942, a public lecture organised by the local committee of the Ministry of Information on *Life in the Soviet Union* was given in Cannons Restaurant in Duke Street[54].

Soon after the move to Hatfield Peverel, Archie was interviewed again for the *Essex Chronicle* on changes to reading habits in the area. He pointed out that numbers of borrowers registered had risen by 4000, which represented a fifty per cent increase. Of the 13000 readers now registered, 3000 were children. People were also spending as much time reading non-fiction as fiction although, as Archie pointed out in a corrective letter the following week, this did not mean people borrowed as many non-fiction books as fiction, but that they took longer to read and required deeper concentration. Biography and travel were the most popular non-fiction subjects, while *Three Men in a Boat* by Jerome K. Jerome was one of the most popular novels. Service personnel billeted in the town were given temporary membership and withdrawn books continued to be donated to local units, as well as to the prison and the YMCA.[55]

Two further problems arose about this time. As Archie said to Phyl, he had a sneaking sympathy for the library caretaker.

"He told the library committee that he'd applied for an Essential Uniforms Certificate from the Board of Trade."

"What's that for, exactly?"

"He hoped it would mean he could get a new uniform without using his clothing coupons. A bit of a nerve, but he works hard."

"What a cheek," said Phyl. "They won't give it to him will they?"

"That's what made me smile; The Board of Trade suggested a distinctive cap or armband, but for a uniform the coupons would have to be spent."

"So what did he do? I'd love to have seen his face at the thought of a distinctive arm-band."

---

54 *Essex Chronicle* Nov 1942
55 *Essex Chronicle* 20th and 27th March 1942

"He wasn't best pleased. Anyway, the committee offered to buy him a new uniform if he surrendered the full quota of coupons[56]. He said he'd have to think about it, so I don't know what he'll do. He does look a bit scruffy at the moment."

A more serious problem was the decision by the Ministry of Health, that having agreed to the funding of the Citizens Advice Bureau for 1941, it could no longer fund it at such a level. Much of the work was already done by volunteers, but there were not enough available to cover for the whole time. The committee agreed that the work was of considerable value to the community. They sought permission for the borough to contribute part of the cost and appoint a temporary library assistant on £150 per annum to carry out the work. A voluntary helper was subsequently offered the post.

The bombing continued throughout the year, with heavy raids on the Hoffmann's factory in July and December 1942. The damage to nearby houses and the resulting death toll put continued pressure on the local people and ensured the casualty officer and the Casualty Information Bureau were kept busy.

Early in 1943, Archie asked the committee for a salary revision. He pointed out that he had reached his maximum of £360 per annum and, in the light of all the extra duties and increasing costs, a revision was justified. A special meeting agreed to pay him an extra increment of £25 for each of the next two years. The library was facing problems with the inability of the bookbinding firms to meet the needs of the library through staff shortages[57]. This was put into perspective in early May, when the worst bomb attack of the war hit Chelmsford[58]. Hoffmann's had already been gutted a month earlier but now more than fifty people were killed and almost a thousand lost their homes. Marconi's works were flattened, while the bus station received a direct hit, as did one of the local schools. Eleven elderly patients were killed when New Hall Hospital was hit.

The library was closed for ten days, as parts of the building were in a dangerous condition. There was extensive superficial damage but furniture and fittings were unaffected, except for the blackout frames and curtains, which had to be completely replaced. The closure and the major disruption throughout the town and its immediate surroundings led to a 10% decline in library usage during the second quarter. Staff at the information centre were praised and thanked for the services they so willingly offered in the

56 Museum and Library Committee Minutes 15th April 1942 p305

57 Museum and Library Committee Minutes 8Feb 1943 p339

58 Begent, Chelmsford at War pp32-43

aftermath of the blitz. The C.A.B. was also out of action for a time as a result of the damage.[59]

Call-up threatens

In the April before this major bombing raid took place, Archie had an underlying worry which he shared with Phyl.

"I got some bad news today," he said.

"Bad news? What now?" said Phyl.

"I'm no longer exempt from military service. The town clerk told me this afternoon."

"Does that mean you'll be called up?" said Phyl. "How long before you go? What are we going to do? What if anything happens to you?" It was Phyl's worst nightmare. Apart from Lil, she had no-one to rely on. She would be alone, with Keith barely two years old and all the problems of rationing, bomb attacks…. It was all too much.

"Obviously I'd prefer to stay and do what I do now," said Archie. "I can't see them finding anyone else to take all that on."

"They must be completely mad to take you away from all that."

"I'd hate to leave you on your own, I really would, but thousands of people are coping," said Archie. "Look at your sister, Madge. Will has been in the RAF right through the Battle of Britain. She's had to cope."

"But you do so much for Chelmsford. What about the casualty work and the C.A.B. and the local committee."

"Well the town clerk has written requesting a deferment on my behalf, so it may not happen just yet.[60]"

In July, Archie was summoned for interview with the District Manpower Commission at Colchester. He was told that his case no longer justified further deferment. The town clerk had immediately written to the board pointing out that in addition to his role as librarian he was engaged in very important work, in which he could not possibly be replaced. He was Officer in charge of the Information and Admin Centre, Casualty Bureau Officer and Emergency Information Officer for the Ministry of Information. The clerk had also written to the Ministry of Health pointing out that Archie was indispensable and a very serious situation would arise if he was not granted deferment.[61]

59 Librarian and Curator report to Borough Council July 1943 p246
60 Borough Council Minutes p342 5th April 1943
61 Borough Council Minutes p345 12th July 1943

Phyl feared the post every day. Archie did his best to calm her; his own workload kept his mind on his immediate duties. He had some relief from the Air Force cadets he trained in the evenings. In September, Archie travelled up to Grange-over-Sands for an ATC Officers' training course in engine maintenance[62] and on his return one of his cadets produced a cartoon. This showed them all busily working away in various situations putting Archie's new information into practice. A month later, to everyone's relief, the town clerk reported that Archie's case was under review at the District Manpower Board and that he had obtained a six-month deferment until March 1944[63].

Campaigns to support the War Effort on the Home Front continued throughout the year. An ingenious means of saving fuel by damping down coal dust and using garden weeds as a binding agent in forming the dampened dust into balls which, when cool, could be used on the fire, won a £2 prize and public praise from Archie in his role as secretary to the local committee of the Ministry of Information. In the summer the 'Wings for Victory' campaign was a great success and 'Holidays at Home' was repeated, with the museum again being popular. Archie's interest in postage stamp history, developed from his early years at Tottenham, led him to welcome the application for a showcase by the local Philately Society.[64]

Another great success was the book salvage campaign in which over 200,000 books were collected, far exceeding the target of 60,000. During this campaign Archie was visited by a lady who had recently lost her husband.

"She said she had some books of her husband's which she no longer wanted but they were in too good a condition to be pulped," Archie explained to Phyl. "So she asked me if I would go round to the house and see what I thought."

"Couldn't she have brought them in? Surely you're far too busy to go traipsing round people's houses."

"She said it would be better if I went round, so I popped in just before I came home. Well, I've never seen anything like it."

"What do you mean? Books are books, aren't they?" said Phyl.

"She showed me into what was either an office or a study, with a very nice glass fronted bookcase, mahogany I think, and pointed to a set of beautiful calf-bound books. She gave me a key to the bookcase and said she'd be downstairs and to call her when I'd finished. I opened the glass-fronted

62 Photo A & L Kingsby Photogaphers, Grange- Over-Sands
63 Borough Council Minutes P349 11th October 1943.
64 Library and Museum Committee Report p345 12th July 1943

door and took out one of the set. The cover was beautifully smooth, very high quality. Then I opened it. I got a real shock. It was full of the most disgusting pornographic illustrations. I checked some of the others and they were all very similar. They ranged from supposed Edwardian sauciness to absolutely disgusting pictures of activities I wouldn't want you to know even existed."

"How revolting! You didn't take them, did you?"

"No, of course not. I went down and told her they were not suitable."

"What did she say?" asked Phyl.

"She said her husband wasn't really a bad man. He was just addicted to that sort of thing. She said she just wanted them out of the house."

"I suggested she put them to salvage and she seemed to accept it was the only answer. I think she had a kind of fondness for them as objects but hated their content."

***

Phyl's mother, Amy Howard, had visited the family at Hatfield Peverel in the autumn of 1943, but by the new year she was suffering from pneumonia. She died on February 14th and the funeral followed a week later. Amy was the youngest daughter of James Toseland, a local politician and temperance supporter from Kettering in Northamptonshire. She had always supported his beliefs and remained teetotal, although her husband, Charles Howard, had enjoyed his drink. He had died in 1930, but not before they had produced seven children. Phyl was one of five girls. Archie and Phyl took the train to Liverpool Street and from there they travelled by bus to Tottenham. The windows and headlights of the buses were louvered in such a way as to prevent the light from being seen easily from above. The buses were painted grey for the same reason. Bomb damage was everywhere along the bus route, but Rosebery Avenue, where they dropped off Keith to be looked after by Archie's parents, was still intact, as was Baronet Grove when they got there.

Chapter Seven

A Turning Point Approaches

The worst raid occurred during the indiscriminate rocket attacks when on 19th December 1944 a factory was hit and over thirty young ladies were killed.

In the library, Archie reported a crisis in the book stock. This had fallen from 13,000 to 7,000 since 1939. Although the book fund allowed for 1,300 new books per year, over 2,000 were withdrawn. Wear and tear increased as numbers declined. A further 2,000 were awaiting rebinding, a process which was rarely available at the time. Purchasing power had declined by 60% since 1939. All this had led to an increase in complaints and a decline in membership. Archie suggested that one way some money could be saved was by dropping the costs of carriage for library inter-lending. Chelmsford already borrowed more than they lent and it would cut down on clerical costs, as many other libraries had found[65].

The Mid-Essex Technical College had asked for the use of a room for reading and would supply seven hundred books if the library would make the total up to a thousand and provide some shelving. As Archie had been appointed the year before as the lecturer in charge of the librarianship course at the college, he was pleased that the request was accepted. This was one small sign of the general perception that the war could end in the foreseeable future. After Stalingrad the Russian army was advancing; the North Africa campaign had been won; and Allied troops were making hard-fought progress in Italy. The Battle of the Atlantic was effectively over and the Royal Air Force was delivering devastating bombing raids on German cities. In various ways people were beginning to feel optimistic about the future. Since the terrible blitz on Chelmsford in the previous May, bombing had never resumed with such intensity. The new threat was the V-1, or doodlebug as it was known. People soon learned that the time to worry was when its engine stopped. Doodlebugs were an increasing threat by the middle of 1944. In mid-June a doodlebug landed in the grassed area next to Chelmsford swimming baths. Fortunately, it was just after six o'clock on a Sunday morning so there was no one in the baths, but a number of people in nearby properties were injured and over five hundred properties were damaged.

---

65 Library and Museum Committee Report P354 10th Feb 1944

Another sign of increasing confidence was the number of G.I. brides. Towards the end of 1943, Chelmsford had seen the first of a series of weddings between local girls and American servicemen. In the following April, Lil's daughter Nadine married G.I. Danny Lobato at St Andrew's Church in Hatfield Peverel. Archie, Phyl and Keith were there. Keith was thrilled to be given a ride in an American army jeep when Danny was around on leave. In March 1946, the whole family gathered at Waterloo Station to see them off, with their little daughter Lynn, on the train to Southampton. They sailed to the United States and settled in California.

Back in Chelmsford, by the middle of 1944, the Channel Island Refugee Society was permitted to meet for two hours in the small lecture room, on the second Sunday of the month, free of charge[66]. By October, the Ministry of Works no longer required tenancy of the reference library, filing room, basement room or the store room used in connection with the borough food office. The committee therefore agreed that the reference library should be restored to full public use as soon as practicable. The borough engineer had invited tenders for the external repainting of the library, but as only one had been received it was agreed to employ direct labour[67].

It was also agreed to provide a book giving comprehensive information as to training, fees and opportunities covering 140 different careers for girls. Although this was funded under the careers and vocational training section of the library, it was closely related to the work of the Citizens Advice Bureau. The regional officer had interviewed Archie as director. The regional office and the national headquarters considered Chelmsford one of the most efficiently run bureaux in the Eastern Region and were interested to see a grant coming from the borough. They thought extra representatives were needed and suggested the Rotary Club, the British Legion and the Y.M.C.A. as organizations to approach. They would also be working closely with the Ministry of Labour Resettlement Advice Centre. They needed to be sure of funding as the workload would increase with the onset of demobilisation and the need would be greater than at any previous time. The council agreed to approach the organisations suggested and set up advisory panels. They deferred a decision on funding and asked Archie to present the proposals at the next council meeting.

With the end of the war apparently in sight and the threat of invasion long gone, Archie suggested to Phyl that at last they could take a family holiday

66 Op Cit p365 10th July
67 Op Cit P367 9th Oct 1944.

that summer.

"It's a lovely idea, but is it safe?" said Phyl.

"I thought we could go to Bournemouth. It's a long time since we saw the sea, and I know how much you miss getting away for a break," said Archie.

"This wretched war has stolen the best years of our lives. Just when we were doing well enough to live comfortably, all this terrible trouble has to hit us. We can never get those years back."

"We're better off than millions of people. Anyway I thought we could do with a complete break and a week or two at the coast might cheer us up."

"It would be lovely. Yes, let's do it."

Archie booked them into a bed and breakfast establishment run by the very strict Mrs Masters. They spent two weeks walking along the front and through the Winter Gardens, lolling on deck chairs on the beach, reading and playing in the sand with Keith, who soon made friends with other little castle builders on the beach.

"This is the first time since the war started that I've felt happy and relaxed," said Phyl, as the fortnight drew to a close.

"We must do it again," said Archie. "It was lovely to be able to bring Keith to the seaside see him playing in the sand. Let's hope the war ends as quickly as the papers are saying."

A Cruel Attack

In the weeks running up to Christmas, there was an upsurge in rocket attacks. In the worst of these the night shift at Hoffmann's Factory had just returned to their benches, after a carol singing service with the Salvation Army Band, when a V-2 rocket landed between the works and Henry Road, which ran alongside. The immediate impact of the blast ignited a 200-gallon paraffin tank, which sent a ferocious fire ball through the assembly benches. Thirty employees were killed instantly. Rescue services were in prompt attendance but, when Archie arrived next morning to collect details of the casualties, he was overwhelmed by the scene.

"They were still sitting there," he said to Phyl later, "all those girls, mostly in their teens and early twenties. A row of charred bodies, still on their seats, baked into position."

"How absolutely awful, Archie. Are you all right?"

"I'll be all right in a minute," he said, but he was openly crying. "What are we going to tell the families? There's one we still can't identify. There'll be a funeral after Christmas. I think they will all be buried in one big grave; nineteen women, mostly young, and ten men."

"It's terrible when the war is supposed to be nearly over," said Phyl.

"They'll bomb us to the very end now they've got these V-2 rockets. Let's hope the Allies reach Berlin before too many more hit us."

Many more rockets landed in the area around Chelmsford in the early part of 1945. The final raid on the town damaged two factory buildings on 23rd February. On 7th May Germany surrendered: the war in Europe was over and celebrations took place throughout the country. In Hatfield Peverel, Arch and Phyl joined everyone from the village across the road at Claydon's Garage. Drink was produced from the Duke of Wellington, music played and everyone danced, sang and cheered. Keith was now four-and-a-half and sat with his friends in the cab of Mr Claydon's breakdown wagon, pretending to drive to the rescue of whatever cars they could find.

That summer, they arranged another family holiday at the coast. This time they took the train to Exmouth and spent a fortnight enjoying the beach, much as they had the previous year in Bournemouth.

The library book stock had declined further during the year and requests from St John's Hospital and from youth centres, through the District Youth Committee, were reluctantly turned down. Archie strongly recommended that in the next financial year £1,000 should be spent on increasing the book stock[68]. Lack of staff meant that the library had to close early on a regular basis. In response to reports of young children misbehaving in the museum, the committee decided that children under five must be accompanied by an adult.

The Citizens Advice Bureau had added Rotary and Y.M.C.A members to its committee and had received a grant towards funding staff. The importance of the organisation, as the war ended, was stressed in a talk by Mrs D. Keeling, an executive committee member of the National Council for Social Services, who emphasised its role as a buffer between government and client in resettling returning service personnel. She added that a course was being run to train C. A. B. staff in aspects of resettlement work. It was recommended that two members attend from each branch[69]. The committee agreed to this, although one of those selected was away sick at the time so Archie was authorised to attend on his own.

The Mid-Essex Technical College began new courses in librarianship in

---

68 Museum and Library Committee Report P373 12th Feb 1945
69 CAB Sub Committee Minutes p375 and following 5th Feb 1945

the new academic year. They asked if Archie could give a series of lectures on Thursday evenings, on the technical aspects of the subject. As Archie was happy to do so, the Library and Museum Committee agreed. By October the librarian and staff were congratulated on the interest taken in the new librarianship courses. It was hoped that this would contribute to resolving the lack of qualified staff available to process the new stock that was beginning to arrive.

Some time to relax

When he was not at work Archie resumed his enjoyment of cycling. With no car since fuel was not available, he would cycle around the Essex countryside on what he called his racing bike. This had slim tyres, drop handlebars and a derailleur gear system.

"You should get a bike," he said to Phyl. "It's lovely just cycling round here. We could even go to Maldon on the bikes."

"I can't balance properly. I'd always be falling off. Besides, if we cycled instead of the bus what would we do with Keith?"

"I've got an idea about that," he said. "I'll make him a little saddle and fix it to my cross-bar."

"How will you do that? Will it be safe?" said Phyl.

"Leave it to me," he said. Later, in the shed, he shaped a piece of wood, took some old vests and a strip of leatherette and made a small saddle which he attached to his crossbar. He would lift Keith and sit him astride the new saddle before setting off down the country lanes.

"Look at those cows," he might shout. He'd stop, take out his Box Brownie camera and take close-up photos of the cows at the field gate. Photography was another hobby. He would darken the kitchen at night and develop the pictures he'd taken.

Archie continued his love of making things in other ways. The shed in the back garden contained his workbench and an impressive collection of wood and metal working tools. In the little spare time he had he would put on his overalls and work away at his latest project. To cope with the power cuts he bought a primus stove and used a large square biscuit tin to contain it. He cut a square of tin out of the side, hinged it and attached a catch so that it made a door. He then placed the stove so that the fuel and wick adjusters were opposite and sat it on his bench to cook the Sunday lunch. Another successful construction was the 'Teasmade' at the bedside. He designed it on the back of a note from the Ministry of Information, and constructed it with an alarm clock which switched on the kettle at the appropriate time. This poured the boiling water into the teapot, while the alarm clock woke them up. His morning cup of tea in bed was guaranteed from then on.

Chapter Eight

The Tottenham Experiment is Born

"He was a man with ideas who, unusually, put them into practice, tested and proved them." Wendy Spink.

"W.J.B. is retiring," said Archie, soon after they returned from Exmouth. "The Tottenham job will be advertised in the next week or so. I would just love to go back there. I'm definitely going to apply."

"That's wonderful; can we move back to Tottenham if you get it?"

"There's a lot of bomb damage. I don't know what the chances are of finding anywhere suitable. Then there's Keith's education. He's only just started at Infant School."

"There must be suitable schools in Tottenham. At least we'll have family there; I can see more of Paulie and Eilie. Keith can get to know his cousins," said Phyl.

"Well, I have to get the job first," said Archie. "They haven't even advertised it yet."

Archie applied and attended for interview on 5th October 1945. He was one of three candidates shortlisted for final interview by the General Purposes Committee and was selected for appointment as Director of Libraries and Museum (temporary).

"Why is it temporary?" said Phyl. "Surely they must know you are the best one for the job. Are you sure you should accept?"

"I suppose they just want to make sure I'm the right person. It's a sort of trial period for a year. That's what I understand by it."

He resigned his post in Chelmsford, but Tottenham Borough Council agreed to Archie continuing to visit and advise there until a replacement had been appointed. At the end of his first year as director, Mac, as he was now known, was the only applicant for the re-advertised permanent post and was reappointed, to the satisfaction of all concerned.

Mr Bennett retired in December, after forty years as librarian at Tottenham. He had welcomed Archie at the start of his career and was clearly delighted to be able to hand over to a person he had helped and encouraged through his early years in the service. He had established an atmosphere of co-operation and friendship amongst the staff and was sure that this had contributed to the efficient running of the libraries and museum. In his final contribution to the staff newsletter, Mr Bennett thanked all concerned with the service during his time in office and the people of Tottenham for their support.

Archie was invited to offer a personal note on taking up the leadership role. He wrote:

Not least of the pleasures of taking up my appointment as Director of Libraries and Museum in succession to my old mentor and friend "W. J. B." is the feeling I have had of 'coming home.' It is twenty years since I first started up the 'stone steps' as a junior and, after an absence of fifteen years, I find T. P. L. changed in many respects, but indelible features (and faces) remain which give to the 'Old Central' a ghostly air. I am looking forward to welcoming those of you who are still away and I can assure you all, both new and old, that I shall aim to ensure the best conditions and the happiest relations among a staff united in their determination to repair the time lost in the war years. Not only will it be necessary to recover the pre-war position but I hope it will be possible to create a new quality in our service to the people of Tottenham. These will constitute no mean tasks which I am confident we shall achieve, for under my predecessor a fine tradition of service has been built up. The sooner we can get down to the job together the better.

Tottenham had suffered heavily from enemy bombing from the first major raid in 1940 through to the final V2 rocket in March 1945. Most children had been evacuated and, in the final months of 1945, a major clear-up operation and the provision of an estate of 'prefabs' in White Hart Lane was underway. Archie's parents in Rosebery Avenue were unharmed. He was able to stay overnight after the monthly committee meetings to save the journey home to Hatfield Peverel. Phyl found these days interminable. She looked forward to his return the following evening but found herself nagging him as soon as he got back.

The Central Library hall had suffered some damage but the engineer's report confirmed its safety. It would need capital expenditure of £100 for repairs and would subsequently need redecoration. Various other blast walls would need to be dismantled. The sandbag walls around Bruce Castle, the only museum in London to remain open throughout the war, had already been removed. A redecoration programme for all the library buildings was needed.

"We are very pleased to welcome our new Director of Libraries and Museum, Mr A.W. McClellan. As many of you know, Mr McClellan began his library career here in Tottenham, and we are delighted to welcome him back to his home territory as the whole nation makes a fresh start after the turmoil of world war." Thus on 3rd January 1946, the chairman of the Library and Public Buildings Committee introduced the new director. Committee members responded with nods and good wishes.

"Thank you, Mr Chairman, and members of the committee," said Mac. "I'm sure my delight at returning, as director to T. P. L., is obvious to all. As Mr Chairman said, our borough is entering a new and exciting time. I would particularly like to thank Mr Bennett for all the advice and helpful suggestions he has passed on during our tour of all the libraries and museum, and for introducing me to all the staff individually."

"At next month's meeting I will present the committee with an outline programme of development for the borough's libraries. In the meantime, there is an immediate need for capital expenditure to repair war damage and for improvements to children's libraries at Central and West Green."

The seven-page development plan was circulated with the papers for the February meeting. The chairman deferred discussion until April, to give members more time to consider the proposals, which on first reading seemed very far-reaching. At the April meeting the paper was officially approved, with a few members expressing reservations. This document was the first comprehensive expression of Mac's revolutionary ideas, which were to transform the library service and dominate the rest of his professional life.

In the immediate future, the issue of staff returning from war duties had to be managed under the Rehabilitation and Re-settlement of Local Government Officers Regulations. One-year courses would be funded for those who had enrolled, but if all the ten expected to return enrolled at once, the libraries would be very short-staffed. The committee therefore agreed that half the group would defer retraining until the first group returned to work. The backlog of work was such that many of the temporary replacements could be absorbed, although some would no doubt leave. Mac was keen to support other members of staff who enrolled for part-time courses in their own time. He persuaded the committee to fund their course fees. Another problem brought to his immediate attention was the difficulty that had arisen through the women cleaners receiving instructions from the male caretaker. Mac's suggestion that a forewoman cleaner be appointed was agreed, interviews carried out, and the post filled.

Mac had stated in his conclusion, that he had put the report together in some haste, but the principles it represented were the result of a great deal of thought and experience, over his twenty years working in public libraries. He clearly distinguished between purpose, function, objectives, and uses. In his view, purpose applies to all libraries: it is *to facilitate the communication process.*

He goes on to define the **function** of a library as:

To acquire and store books and printed material, and to organise the material in such ways as to enable any of the material to be readily available to users.

The underlying principle of Mac's thinking was that the reader and not the book should be the priority of the public library. This was a contentious theory in the first half of the twentieth century. Libraries had not been set up in response to public demand, but by Victorian and Edwardian philanthropists who wished to bring education and improvement to the lower classes. As late as 1934, the Library Association Record published an article stating that:

'Public libraries should have the best books and then find readers for them.'

Their benefactors had originally seen public libraries as a service to the public, not a commercial enterprise, and therefore impervious to changing demands. As the quote above illustrates, the quality of the reading matter in the eyes of the professional librarians was the key criterion. This inevitably led to the values of people from educated backgrounds influencing book selection, generally in favour of the humanities. Scientific and technical subjects were not considered to be culturally significant and were therefore less well represented.

Some librarians had acknowledged the need to go some way towards meeting wider requirements, but no coherent methodology had been put into practice. Mac argued that, with the more egalitarian age developing after the 1945 election, and the implementation of the 1944 Education Act, there would be an increasing need and demand for a wider range of books. If public libraries were to contribute to the post-war recovery and justify their allocation of public money from the rates, they were going to have to offer rather more than a stuffy selection of literature of interest only to a minority. In order to serve the population of the borough the whole system would have to change. The basic elements of these changes were contained in the plan approved at the committee meeting in April 1946.

If the readers were to be served well, there was a need to understand their requirements. The plan involved engaging Mass Observation to conduct a survey of the whole population of the borough. In addition, the book stock had to be more accessible. The plan suggested that the library should be more open plan; that it should shelve and label books in ways that the public could immediately relate to; and that librarians should be retrained to become advisers in specific subject areas. This would involve the reorganisation and refurbishment of the central library and the five branch libraries within the borough. Accessibility applied beyond the library as well as within it. Thus a system was agreed of providing disabled or elderly people, who could not easily leave their homes, with a regular delivery to the door, and was introduced before the end of 1946. At the same time, a service was provided for the Prince of Wales General Hospital. Mac based the scheme on his previous successful hospital service in Chelmsford. The hospital authorities agreed to appoint an honorary librarian from their staff. This enabled a service, on the same terms as the libraries, to operate for patients and nurses.

Reaching children and working with schools involved the provision of mobile libraries, which could also be used two evenings a week in areas of the borough where access to the central or branch libraries was difficult. The mobile library service agreed in the development plan in April 1946 was at the planning stage three years later. The articulated vehicles were very large and an issue arose as to where they could be safely garaged and maintained. The Libraries and Public Buildings Committee learned that a fire station in the borough was no longer in use and could be made available. By July 1949, the vehicles were approaching readiness. Mac had worked with the Borough Education Officer to involve local schools in the programme, but there were areas of the borough where the service would be available to adults. Councillors and officers were asked to identify suitable sites.

At the December meeting, Mac reported that the service would be ready to start in early January 1950. Members of the committee felt that the mayor should be asked to officiate at the formal opening. It soon became clear that the vans would not be ready in January. At the March meeting, Mac reported that the vehicles were now expected by the end of the month.

Mac sought the committee's help in the detailed organisation of the launch. A suitable site would be required, as the vehicles were very large. The mayor would need a rostrum from which to conduct the ceremony, and light refreshments would be needed. The Lido and Baths Committee was approached, and permission was granted to use the lido parking area between the hours of 6.00pm and 8.00pm on 26th April. The Entertainments and Catering Committee was approached to ascertain whether a suitable rostrum could be borrowed for the evening. It was reported that they were happy to give permission, but it would be the responsibility of the Public Libraries and Buildings Committee to provide the means of transporting the rostrum.

After some discussion, the Finance Committee agreed to the expenditure of £10 for light refreshments. The discussion centred on how the sum should be entered in the accounts. It was finally agreed that it should be charged to *other civic expenses*.

Everything now seemed in place. The scheme was launched with great fanfare and the rostrum safely returned. The service formally began on 1st May 1950. The vans served schools during the day and three areas of the borough twice a week between 6.00pm and 8.00pm.

A last-minute hitch occurred when the schools discovered the books were stamped with labels for Tottenham Public Libraries. They insisted that the books should be labelled as the property of Middlesex County Council. In his next director's report, Mac was able to reassure members of the committee that a workable compromise had been reached, and that the service was running well. The schoolchildren loved the service and flocked to the vans whenever they appeared. Thus, the aims of easier access and instilling a love of reading from an early age received a big boost in the borough.

Within two years, all schools in the borough were using the scheme. With the co-operation of teachers it ran very smoothly, but its popularity caused one problem, for which Mac sought the help of the Middlesex Education Committee in solving. The deterioration of the book stock was becoming serious, as there was not enough money to pay for the rebinding of tatty and worn-out books. The Education Committee had repeatedly refused to increase the allowance to cover this expenditure, although Mac had given them a detailed breakdown of costs.[70] At their next meeting the Buildings and Public Libraries Committee offered support to the Borough Council in any representations they might make to the County Council for an increase in the grant[71]. Three months later, both parties reached an agreement.

***

In June 1946, Mac was delighted to see his old colleague and friend from his previous time at Tottenham, Walter Preston, return from war service eager to resume his career. Mac realised that Walter would immediately grasp the need to understand the detailed reading interests and abilities of

---

70 Letter to Education Committee, Director's report June 1953.
71 P. B. L. C. Minutes July 1953

the community as laid down in the agreed plan. He was, therefore, just the man to liaise with the Mass Observation team and he did so to excellent effect. The survey set out to discover the reading habits of the inhabitants of the borough and how these related to their other activities. In particular, the survey wanted to establish their attitude to the public library. The interviewers began by finding out how important people felt the habit of reading was to them, how much reading they did and whether they read magazines, newspapers or books, or any combination of these.

Once the book readers were identified, they were interviewed as a group to establish if they had anything in common and were different in other ways from non-readers. Readers were then asked where they obtained their reading matter. Those using the public library formed a smaller group again subject to further study. They were compared to the non-users to establish what kept people away from the library and to get their views on the library as a service to the public.

A further analysis was made of people's tastes in reading, including fiction, non-fiction, newspapers and magazines, and how their interests matched the library's provision. Finally, readers were consulted about their use of the public library service. They were asked how often they visited the library; whether they used and valued the assistance of the librarians; and what suggestions they had for improvements to the service. It was hoped the survey would show how much the library meant to Tottenham and its individual inhabitants.

All those surveyed were grouped according to age, sex, marital status, occupation, educational level, social class and distance from a public library. In this way, a precise knowledge of the interests and reading abilities of the whole community was achieved. This in turn informed a new approach to book selection based on levels of readability, accuracy, content and social value. Bringing these two aspects together would work towards the objective of matching appropriate books with appropriate readers.

Thus, the delivery services for the elderly and hospitals, and the mobile libraries, were but a small part of the full plan that Mac envisaged for the Tottenham Libraries and Museum over the next few years.

Chapter Nine

Service in Depth

- *And Mak-Lel-Lan, the chief, pondered many things in his heart. And he summoned unto him his wise men and magicians:*
- *And Mak-Lel-Lan told them of a strange and subtile design: Behold, it is written in the book of the World of Libraries.*
- *And they were filled with Wonder.*
- *And he saith: Lo, it shall be called Service in Depth; …*
- *And they rejoiced because of it.*[72]

As this good-humoured extract from the staff journal records, Mac introduced fundamental changes in the organisation and duties of library staff, and in the layout of the library, in order to deliver what became known as *Service in Depth*. This involved retraining and re-grading, but also the introduction of new technology and changes in procedure to free up staff time for the better use of their professional knowledge in the provision of a vastly improved service to the public. In May 1946, he put his proposals to the committee in general terms. In particular, he pointed out that the new grading into junior, intermediate and senior posts as recommended by the Library Association, would simplify the re-grading of scales he would put forward at the next meeting. He gave an assurance that he would consider individual employees with great care in terms of length of service and experience[73].

Mac's next move was to set up a departmental working committee, which included representatives from all sections, to ensure the smooth working of all the department's activities, and to provide a channel for suggestions for improving the service. The staff involved in the first monthly meeting responded positively to the idea of regular consultation.[74]

He also took advantage of a recruitment scheme introduced by the borough council. This involved creating a pool of trainees from students of school leaving age with general schools or matriculation certificates. The students were trained, as a group, in the various aspects of library work so that, as vacancies occurred, they could be filled from the trainees.[75] In December 1949, the county council offered subsistence grants for those

72 Extract from the staff journal, 1948
73 Director's Report, May 1946
74 Director's Report Nov 1946
75 London Letter, June 1947

trainees selected to complete a full-time professional course with the Library Association. This encouraged them to mix with students from a wide range of libraries and so broaden their knowledge and understanding of the profession and bring valuable expertise back to Tottenham.[76]

****

Although library book stocks no longer consisted only of what the librarian thought suitable, they were still arranged as if all readers knew what they wanted and had a serious purpose in mind. Books were therefore shelved, in the case of non-fiction, in the rigid classification of the Dewey system, and alphabetically by author in the fiction section. Mac's study of reader habits and intentions led him to emphasise that the same reader may want a book to further his work or education, another for a light relaxing read, and yet another to follow a hobby or passing interest. Two key changes emerged from this insight.

Firstly, the layout of the library was completely reorganised. On entry, readers would see displays of recent acquisitions, notices of meetings and events and any especially topical issues. Immediately beyond would be the lending library, with light reading the most easily accessible. Beyond this area would be the reference library, with facilities to sit and study. Readers would also be able to seek help and guidance from professional staff particularly expert in the subject area of interest. Mac would have liked a new building designed to provide such a layout from the outset, but he had to adapt the central library, with internal changes and added extensions over time, and adjust the model accordingly. In 1950, he described this new layout as follows:

Its essential feature will be the natural and unimpeded movement from the conditions appropriate to the 'escapist' and 'relaxing' type of interest through to those most appropriate to the more intensely 'specific'. Such an arrangement might be termed 'Service in Depth'.[77]

The other change was in the role and training of staff. As the library service had developed and its book selection, cataloguing and classification had become more centralised, the professional librarians tended to be out of sight in the back rooms dealing with these aspects of running the library. This left unqualified assistants to work at the service desks. This led in turn to librarians being held in low regard. Mac attended a conference of

---

76 Director's Report Dec 1949
77 Library World 52 April 1050. As quoted by Wendy Spink.

the local branch of the Library Association in October 1948 at which he was greatly encouraged by a widely supported paper on the possibility of developing two types of staff, professional and clerical, with promotion open to both, and training to develop the assistants' outlook and enthusiasm. The following year, Mac set up a training scheme in which approved trainees would attend Library School to gain professional qualifications, and an exchange system with nearby libraries whereby two librarians of the same rank would exchange places for a month to broaden their experience. Although several adjacent boroughs showed interest in the scheme, only Hornsey library took part in the first year. The chief librarian of Hornsey wrote full of enthusiasm for the outcomes for his staff and showed a desire to continue with the scheme[78].

Professional librarians took responsibility for particular subject areas and maintained an up-to-date bibliography of their subject. They were no longer confined to the back rooms but available to the reading public to advise and answer questions as required. The boost this gave to morale, and to the quality of service, was expressed in two letters from readers.[79]

Mr Woodley, the headmaster of Rowland Hill Secondary School, explained that he was due to give a lecture at the London University Law School and needed a particular book published in 1930. He had tried new and second-hand book shops, university libraries and several government departments. In despair, he came into the Tottenham Central Library and, after ten days, an assistant informed him that the book had arrived. He could not have been more grateful.

A Miss Sambridge gave more general praise to the staff for their friendly, helpful approach and appropriate guidance to the elderly, directing them to the books they would particularly enjoy.

Mac passed on these compliments at the regular staff meetings and told the staff that the committee would see copies of the letters. He thanked them for their continuing commitment to their readers.

***

Mac was always on the lookout for ways to use technical equipment to free staff to use their skills to full effect. In May 1946, he reported that he had obtained a second-hand postage-franking machine for £30. The cost of a new one was £63.10s. This bargain would save 40,000 handwritten items per year, release three quarters of the hours of one full-time assistant,

---

78 Director's Report Apr 1951
79 Director's report May 1947

obviate the need for postage stamps and thereby eliminate licking.[80] In December 1946, he requested permission to invest in a key punch and verifier to provide a more comprehensive analysis of the readers and their needs. It would reduce the annual cost of stationery by approximately one third and a free three-week training course would be provided.[81] In June 1947, he sought permission to hire, at £12.00 a month, a 38-column punched card counter sorter. This would sort the punched cards into any categories and count them at the same time, which would enable rapid analysis of the cards in every possible combination[82].

Meanwhile, in the previous month, Mac had sought permission to purchase a Rectophot Photostatic cabinet, a form of photocopier. This was to provide a new service particularly for students and teachers, at a time when so many books required for serious study were obtainable only for short periods or for reference. Users would pay a small charge to cover materials used. Only six major libraries in the country provided such a service at the time.[83] A dark room was fitted out, a copyright form printed off, and charges agreed for both a negative print and a subsequent positive copy.[84] By the end of the following month, the demand for the use of the photostat machine was so great that Mac asked for the committee's support in using his discretion over which items could be copied. As *The Evening News* reported, it would only be used for educational or cultural purposes.[85] By January 1949, a new camera and an enlarger were added and, for presentations, a new autoscope was agreed as a replacement for an old silent cine-projector.

A further piece of equipment was provided after agreement in September 1949. Up to this point, newspapers had been bound in yearly volumes. They required a large area of storage space and put pressure on staff, who had to locate the volume or volumes requested and manhandle them into the reference area. Mac proposed that all this could be dispensed with through the provision of a microfilm copy. The copies could then be read with a microfilm reader and the storage system and binding could be abandoned[86].

Binding was a process that gave Mac increasing concern. As he pointed out to the committee, the bookbinding contractors had increased prices

<hr>

80 Director's report May 1946
81 Director's report Dec 1946
82 Director's Report June 1947
83 Director's report May 1947
84 Director's report Oct 1947
85 Evening News 20 February 1948
86 Director's report Sept 1949

by 110% compared with their pre-war charges[87]. In order to stay within budget limits, a backlog of 4,000 books was awaiting rebinding and the number was increasing each month. With the committee's agreement, Mac researched the possibilities of an in-house bindery and, in his report for January 1949, he offered a detailed and costed proposal for the accommodation of a bindery, equipment required, staffing provision and estimates for set-up and running costs. The St Anne's branch offered the best base for accommodating the bindery. It had a suitable room and would need only minor changes. Equipment posed more of a problem as most of the machines required were unobtainable as new and unused. Mac nevertheless felt confident that the scheme could be up and running from the beginning of the financial year in April[88].

At this time, the town clerk submitted proposals for a centralised printing establishment. It was obvious to Mac that it made sense to combine the printing with the binding at the St Anne's branch. He suggested that a room next to the proposed bindery could be converted for the purpose with minimal difficulty and cost. He added that further substantial savings could be made by having the two inter-related processes working together.[89] Although this was agreed and the setting-up put in motion, there were delays over obtaining some items of equipment and in recruiting suitable staff. Mac had to seek permission to increase pay to above union minimum rates before any suitably qualified candidates applied[90]. There were also delays in fitting out the printing room. The key to productivity, Mac told the committee, is in the arrangement of operations and the organisation of work methods. Hull Public Library had been running a bindery along similar lines for some years, and it was there that he went to learn how to make the most of the new facility. By the end of September, he was able to report that both binding and printing services had overcome their initial problems and were already saving a considerable percentage compared with commercial costs. The services had received many compliments and no complaints[91]. Mac was particularly pleased to be invited to describe the setting-up and working of the bindery at the 1949 Annual Library Association Conference.

By June 1950, eight months later, the bindery was working at full stretch and saving costs per book rebound. Gold lettering was provided for

87 Director's report Feb 1948
88 Director's report Jan 1949
89 Director's Report Apr 1949
90 Director's Report June 1949
91 Director's special report Sept 1949

many more. The printing section had also worked very well, with further savings compared to the outsourced service. With typical thoroughness, Mac supplied detailed figures on costs, number of books bound and items printed, and suggestions for two more machines, which would speed both processes up and save further costs. A vari-type machine, awaiting delivery, would minimise the cost of print items needed in small numbers. Currently the metal plates used in printing had to be ordered from outside suppliers. This often delayed production by as much as a fortnight. Mac provided estimates for the purchase of the equipment required. It would make the operation self-sufficient and, when everything was in place, the combined sections would save approximately £1,500 a year. He also gave precise figures on the extra hours bindery workers spent in the printing section and sought permission to recruit an additional male binder, and a female operative learner, directly from school leavers[92].

A year later, when the bindery had been running for a full two years, the backlog of books awaiting rebinding had been all but cleared. The printing output had increased in quantity and variety. The council minutes made heavy demands through timescale and delivery to members. The vary-typing machine was in constant use in the production of the minutes, so a second machine was required. The metal plate production was hampered by technical difficulties but produced 75% of what was required. Operators' experience was improving the success rate and Mac had no doubt that it would soon be fully operational. Such had been the growth of the sections that the accommodation was too small and for effective communication the unit should be at the central library. Until an extension was built the cramped conditions would hold it back[93]. A further year later Mac summarised the benefits of the sections: a major financial saving, a reliable supply of paper through bulk purchase and the ability to use paper off-cuts, which would remain with the printer if the jobs were outsourced[94].

***

The Libraries and Public Buildings Committee accepted further changes at their meeting of April 1947. These involved an extension of the loan period from two to three weeks, the abolition of fines for children's loans and of the fees for registration and renewal of membership. Mac had found the temporary extension of the loan period in Chelmsford to be effective. In Tottenham, by far the heaviest borrowing and return activity was on

---

92 Director's report Feb 1950
93 Director's Report Sept 1951
94 Director's report Oct 1952.

Saturdays, as it was often the only time when people at work could visit the library. If circumstances prevented their visit, they could well end up having to pay a fine through situations beyond their control. He also felt that the library should be a service that was open and free to all those who wanted to use it. There should be no cost to join or formal membership. The committee agreed with his approach and confirmed the changes.[95] These resulted in a reduction in overdue books. By March 1951, the new system had settled down but there was still a need to send fifteen thousand recovery letters in the year. In some cases a librarian had to visit the home in an attempt to recover the book. In these circumstances Mac proposed a doubling of fines after the first overdue week. This could act as a stronger deterrent, and would raise the annual income by some £200[96].

***

Mac had stated in his *Programme of Development* the importance of the regular daily transporting of books from one branch to another so that readers' needs were rapidly met. A commercial firm had provided this service before the war, but had reduced deliveries to twice weekly. A daily service was necessary to meet the needs of readers quickly enough to save the purchase of extra copies of the books in demand. He proposed the purchase of a suitable van to make these deliveries. It could also be used for hospital and homebound readers and for transporting stationery and general supplies to branch libraries. The caretaker at Coombes Croft Branch was underemployed and an experienced driver with a Safety First Medal. If he were employed as a part-time driver, no additional staff would be required. Mr Cox, the caretaker, was keen to take up the role. In March 1946, Mac reported that a suitable van, in good condition, was available and, as it had been written off, it would cost nothing. Once ownership had been transferred and the rebranding and minor repairs had been carried out, it would be ready for service[97]. The committee agreed to the acquisition and that the necessary conversion should take place. Within the month,[98] all was ready, the driver's pay rate agreed and the van began its daily deliveries.

***

Early in 1950, Mac reported to the committee that the Library Association had prepared a leaflet entitled, *A Centenary of Public Library Service*, which

---

95 LPBC Mins1692 Apr 1947
96 Director's report Mar 1951
97 Director's Report Mar 1946
98 Director's Report Apr 1946

was available for circulation. It was intended to stimulate Local Authorities to assess their current library services. Mac said that he was available to answer any questions they may have. In July, Mac explained to the committee that the London and Home Counties Branch of the Library Association would be holding a National Book Exhibition at the headquarters of the National Book League in September. Part of the exhibition would require local libraries to provide some supervision. Mac nominated Mr Fenton for two days later in September. He planned some events in the Tottenham Libraries to coincide with the exhibition, including the usual Children's Book Week, and he asked for £20 to be available for him to entertain important national, and international, visitors.

In May, Mac received a letter from P. H. Newby of the BBC Talks Department inviting him to give a talk on the centenary. Newby advised that, to avoid the possibility of boring the Home Service listeners, Mac should focus on the reading habits of the public, quoting from his own experience, and perhaps move towards the historical perspective towards the end. He invited Mac to phone him to discuss the matter further. He also understood that Mac would be on holiday in South Wales at the time, so suggested he could make the broadcast from Cardiff.

After a brief telephone conversation in response to the invitation, Mac pondered the issues before writing a detailed response. He pointed out that book serialisations and reviews already had their followers. What was needed, he suggested, was a recognition that, as well as reading for leisure, many people used books, not for their own sake, but as 'tools' to help them find out or do something. He cited evidence from the recent Mass Observation Survey in Tottenham, and quoted a number of enquiries at the library to illustrate the point. He went on to suggest a regular programme, divided into two parts. The first part would draw attention to recently published books, which could be of use to a variety of people needing to learn about or do something. The content of the books would be outlined, but not reviewed, and their readability mentioned. The second section would answer listeners' queries on books that would suit their particular purpose. The programme might also include an interview with a listener who had submitted a query of specific interest. He would be encouraged to explain how he had become involved in the activity and how the recommended book had proved helpful. Mac gave the example of a recent request for a book illustrating a 'lover's knot'. He discovered, after meeting the request, that it was required by a confectioner who wanted it as a design on a wedding cake.

Mac suggested that this would stimulate a latent interest in a wide range of books and in the role of the library in providing helpful information and guidance. The ideas clearly caught P. H Newby's imagination. He circulated the suggestions widely within the BBC. Only the single talk from Cardiff on 17th August resulted from this, although this was repeated on the Overseas Service at the end of the month.

In August, the family drove down to Swansea to stay with Leslie Rees, the chief librarian of Swansea Libraries, and his wife Evelyn. They took Keith on the tram along to The Mumbles, and had days at Port Einon and Oxwich Bay. Leslie and Evelyn were good hosts who provided a relaxing break. Mac could not relax completely, however. He worked through the typed script of his pending broadcast, mindful of the reminder to make it interesting. After lunch with their hosts, on Thursday 17th August, Mac set off for Cardiff clutching the sheaf of papers containing his talk.

"Good Luck, Mac," said Leslie and Evelyn Rees together.

"Speak clearly, Arch. We'll all be listening," said Phyl.

"Good Luck, Dad," said Keith.

On arrival Mac was welcomed into the studio and shown the set-up. He was glad of a cup of tea before the rehearsal. He felt confined and was reminded to speak into the microphone, and not look down at his script. Soon everything was arranged and the countdown began.

"Our talk this evening is *The Library and You* and our speaker is Mr A. W. McClellan, Director of Libraries and Museum for the London Borough of Tottenham." said the announcer. "He is speaking on the occasion of the centenary of the passing of the first General Public Libraries Act."

"During the last thirty years," Mac began, "we have seen an astonishing increase in all kinds of leisure activities, such as the use of the motor car, the radio, and now the television. Millions listen to the same radio programmes, read the same newspapers, go to the same films and millions will shortly be watching the same television programmes.

Films are so expensive to produce that they must be easy to understand, and must not offend anyone. It is widely known that films produced for worldwide distribution are made for an audience with a mental age of thirteen years. Radio programmes in the United States are sometimes assessed by a *programme-analyser*. The programme is tested on a small scientifically selected audience and anything they dislike is removed before the broadcast.

If we look more closely into other ways people spend their leisure time," continued Mac, "we shall see that roughly the same number who visit the cinema once a week, about half the adult population, are regular readers of books. In the thirty years since 1920, the number of regular readers has increased six fold to twelve million people. Although most people read books for relaxation and entertainment, many also read to extend their knowledge and understanding." Mac quoted examples from the recent Mass Observation of reading in Tottenham to illustrate the range and variety of subjects the librarians had been asked about. These ranged from *the making of an Anglo-German concertina*, to *mink farming*.

"Books have other advantages," he went on, " you can read at your own pace, look back to remind yourself of something or, as a child said to me, 'I like books best 'cos I can read them in bed.' In particular, as authors of books do not have to satisfy such vast audiences, they are free to write about new ideas or views that some may reject or find offensive. So, although we may not like some of what is written, we have to get used to new ideas. Without this we wouldn't be able to live together at all. Books guarantee the expression of minority views, which other forms of mass information tend to discourage.

The Mass Observation Survey revealed that people who read books regularly were more interested and active than non-readers. In particular, they were more interested in radio, films, newspapers, music, foreign affairs, politics, games, religion, social work and dancing. Non-readers were more interested in football pools, pubs, horse racing and dog racing. Thus the encouragement of wide reading is important, as books provide one of the essential means of forming our own independent views. They can help us acquire the habits of critical thinking and tolerance of the views of others.

That brings me to the main point of this talk," said Mac. "The special part played by our nationwide system of public libraries. This service is easily the greatest single source of books in this country. Through a system of voluntary mutual co-operation between libraries, every reader has access to more than forty million books. Interested citizens have free access to facilities for reading books of every field of knowledge, expressing every point of view. Lack of wealth is no barrier to knowledge or information."

Mac concluded the talk by pointing out the vital contribution to the maturity of outlook that the public library service had made to the country and the pride we could take in the Centenary of the first General Public Libraries Act. He hoped he had been able to show that the somewhat silent service had a serious role as well as its contribution to pleasure and relaxation.

"As a parting thought," he added, "may I remind you that the Nazis were fully aware of this serious role of libraries, so much so that one of their first acts, upon seizing power, was to ransack the libraries of Germany and publicly burn thousands of books, even before falling upon their political and racial opponents?"

Back in Swansea, Phyl gave Mac a big hug. "Well done, Arch," she said. "It was loud and clear, and really interesting."

"Yes, well done, Mac. You really brought it to life." said Leslie Rees, passing him a glass of scotch and water. "Congratulations! Raise your glasses, ladies." They all raised their glasses. Keith had been watching them and raised his glass of lemonade. "Well done, Dad," he said apeing the grown-ups. Once back home in Hatfield Peverel, sorting through the pile of mail delivered in their absence, Mac came across a letter from his old headmaster at Risley Avenue School, James Williams. Mr Williams was now so ill that he was attended by a nurse night and day. He had scribbled the letter in pencil and asked his daughter to rewrite it in ink on his behalf. He had heard Archie's talk and wrote:

It gives me great pleasure to know of the solid character and varied achievements of my old boys. I send my warmest greetings and wishes for truest success to a very worthy old scholar.

Mac was touched by the letter. He wrote thanking his old headmaster and hoping his health improved.

Tottenham: Service in Depth

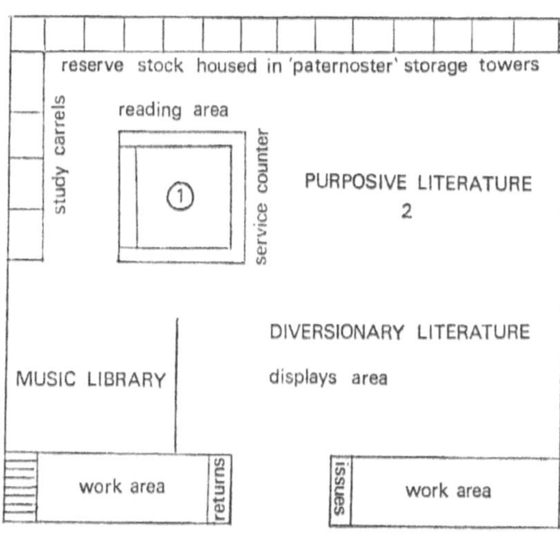

Schematic diagram (non-proportional and not to scale) of 'service in depth' arrangement.

1. The central staircase leads up from the service counter to the Bibliographal Department, which is arranged under subject divitions - cataloguing, classification, stock revision, suggestions, requests. Alternative access is by staircase at bottom left.

2. Reference and loan material is shelved in a single sequence.

Mac welcomes Vera Brittain

Mac 1946

Mobile Library
in Action

Family in 1950s

1955

On Holiday in Wales, 1950

Visit to German Libraries

Further Tottenham Pictures

Information for readers

Proclamation of Queen Elizabeth II,
Town Hall Tottenham

Bruce Castle

Keith's degree celebration, Lampeter.
June 1962

Rosemount, Llanon

Arch's grandfather clock

Arch & Phyl in retirement

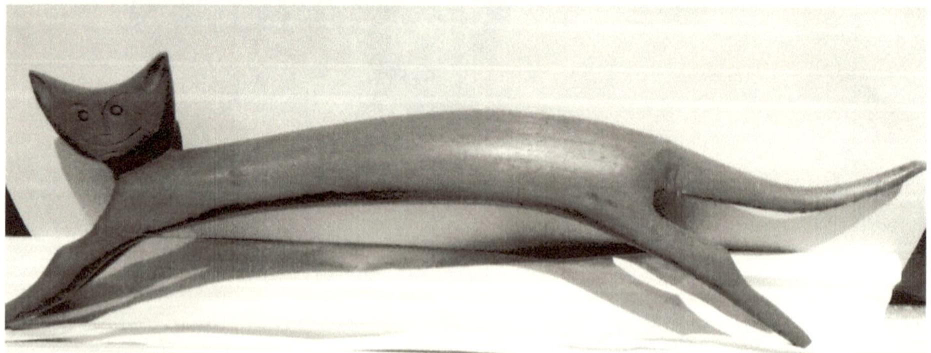

And his cat

Chapter Ten

Encouraging the Reading Habit

"The foundation of good reading habits is best developed in childhood".[99]
A.W. McClellan.

In his experience, from his own childhood and that of his son, Mac felt that a love of reading, and a regular habit of reading that developed from it, was of great benefit to the individual. He believed that libraries had a vital role to play in encouraging this in children. The agreed programme of development stated that this aspect of the service needed substantial improvement. Key needs were: improved accommodation; trained staff; close co-operation with schools; and a senior assistant, trained and experienced in working with children, to take charge of all children's work. He had been involved in various ways with schools and children at Penge and at Chelmsford, and soon established links with the schools in the Borough of Tottenham.

The development of the mobile library system, described earlier, was a major step in providing access for children, but it was also used by adults in outlying areas of the Borough. Similarly, extension services would ideally be available to interest and inform everyone in the borough. These would take various forms, including lectures, readings by well-known authors, information on relevant new publications provided to societies and factories, and relevant displays in the central library and branches.

***

In May 1946, five schoolchildren from Tottenham had their pictures selected for display in the Royal Drawing Society's annual exhibition of children's work. The Society agreed to loan the exhibition to Tottenham public library for two weeks in June and July. Mac suggested that the pictures be hung in the central library hall[100].

In October 1946, Mac proposed to the committee the first Children's Book Week. By holding a two-week event in the main hall of the central library, he hoped to arouse the interest of local schoolchildren in the public libraries. With the full co-operation of the borough education officer, classes were encouraged to attend a series of talks by well-known children's authors. The National Book League supplied an attractive display of children's books and assisted with recruiting speakers; costs were estimated at £30.

99 A Programme of Development for the Tottenham Public Libraries. A.W.M Feb 1946, p.5
100 Director's Report May 1946

The week took place in February 1947. The main book display was set up in the central library, with smaller displays in each of the four branch libraries. From the Monday to the Friday, two morning and two afternoon sessions were held, at which well known authors spoke and the film *Chapter and Verse*, on loan from the National Book League, was shown. The Saturday was an open day with a quiz in the morning and a puppet show in the afternoon. Two competitions were organised. Children were invited to submit an essay describing what they appreciated about the library and how they would like the service improved. There were seventy-six entries, all of a good standard. An analysis of the essays produced a most useful list of suggestions and criticisms. A painting competition for the design of a book jacket produced 186 paintings, which were subsequently displayed at a suitable time. Mac was delighted with the response. Over four thousand children attended and five hundred new readers enrolled. On the day after the event, over one thousand books were issued from the children's section of the central library. The children's librarian was quite taken aback by a group of children who approached her and announced they had formed a committee, with an elected chairman and secretary, which would meet at the library to discuss and suggest ideas for the future of the children's section. Mac stated that the event had been an outstanding success, the staff involved had worked with enthusiasm, and he intended that it should become an annual event[101].

Further activities for children included film displays at the central library, and story hours at the central and branch libraries. Children were invited to participate in various competitions following the book cover painting success. These included bringing something they had made at home, further essays and a wide range of others devised by the senior children's librarian over the following years. In September 1950, the theme of the book week displays was the centenary of the Public Libraries Act. Children's favourite reads in 1850 formed the main display in the central library and the branch libraries had similar themes. The usual activities took place but, in addition, the children's play-reading group put on a play and a pantomime to packed audiences in the central library hall. Schools' interest continued to grow with 1,500 children visiting in school groups and many more children signing up as readers. Most of the teenagers who had shown an interest in the events and displays felt they were too old for a Children's Library. Mac suggested that, when it became possible, there should be a young people's room to act as a bridge between the children's and adult sections.[102]

101 Director's Report March 1947
102 Director's Report Oct 1950

Mac's keen support for improved provision for and involvement of children in the library was continued with his son, Keith, at home.

"His teacher says he's very bright," he said. "He's reading well and learning fast. I think we should get him tested for intelligence. We can see how he compares across the board. Not just in Hatfield."

"Are you sure it's a good idea? Where will you take him? He's used to school and his teacher. We don't want to frighten him, or make him feel as if he's failed something," said Phyl.

"There's a place in London, Wimpole Street. It's the National Foundation for Educational Research."

"No, Arch, it sounds terrifying for a little six-year-old. I'm sure he'll be frightened out of his wits."

"They do special intelligence tests; it's a really friendly atmosphere. I'm sure he'll enjoy it."

He took Keith for the assessment and was delighted to discover from the various tests Keith was given that his son had an I.Q of 130 and was described as a cheerful extrovert type with a good deal of drive and a fair amount of aggression. The consultant summed him up as a boy with the intellectual and temperamental qualities to do very well, provided he had sufficient competition[103]. Mac was encouraged by this report to provide Keith with a constant supply of books to read. He was happy to support his son's love of *Biggles* and *Just William*, as well as Arthur Ransome's *Swallows and Amazons* series, but he also brought him new children's fiction. He refused comics except *The Eagle* and later bought him the *New Elizabethan* magazine.

***

For adults, a series of lectures at the central library and at the Devonshire Hill and West Green branches was planned for the autumn and winter of 1946-7. These included talks on emigration to various countries in what was to become the Commonwealth, musical themes, botanical and gardening topics, among others. At the end of June in 1946, the organisers of Tottenham Farm Week invited the library, at short notice, to set up a temporary branch and display at their exhibition. An excellent effort was made and the display evoked a lot of interest and a large number of enquiries about the library service[104].

---

103 Report from the National Foundation for Educational Research.
104 Director's Report July 1946

Some of the lectures at the branch libraries were poorly attended. Mac proposed to the committee that it would be worth showing films of an educational or cultural nature, especially those not widely shown in commercial cinemas. He reported that he had included an estimate for a cine-projector in the following year's budget. The committee approved the new arrangements as the films had been much more popular than the lectures. At the same meeting, the committee reported that they had received a request for political talks from across the political spectrum, but had refused on the grounds that the political groups were best placed to organise these for themselves[105].

***

At their July 1947 meeting, the committee expressed their thanks for the impressive *Report to the People*, which Mac had produced. They agreed to his request that a function be organised to include a pictorial display of the work of the department, a short film show and lecture, with printed copies of the report available for the public. Invitations were to be extended to distinguished persons in the borough and suitable refreshments provided.

As a result of the success of the first three seasons of lectures, films and exhibitions, Mac sought to develop the policy so that each library became the cultural centre for its area. The successful play-reading group could be a model for a group for listening to and discussing music played on a gramophone. One could be purchased for £35. Although this was agreed in principle, the purchase was continually delayed. A frustrated resident wrote complaining that he had located an alternative record library in Walthamstow, only to be told that it was for the use of residents of Walthamstow only.[106] A further letter six months later requested the setting up of a library of language records, as the Linguaphone sets were very expensive. Mac suggested to the committee that a limited record library of language records in French, German and Spanish would be affordable[107]. After another year, the Edmonton library launched a full record library. This was publicised in the local press and led to even further pressure from residents[108]. Early in 1954, the rules and conditions of use were agreed with the town clerk and language records were made available[109].

In October 1954, Mac responded to a renewed interest in the proposed

105 LPBC Mins Dec1946 p 1139
106 Letter copied in Director's report July 1950
107 Letter copied in Director's report January 1950
108 Letter copied in Director's report February 1952
109 Director's Report Feb 1954

gramophone library, reminding the committee that the estimates he had originally presented to them were now five years old and had been overtaken by events. In particular, 78rpm records were no longer produced in any numbers as long-playing records (LPs) had become the norm. He suggested that the library should be restricted to LPs. Another issue was that of space. The central library was already very short of space and, as a gramophone would be required for occasional checks on possible damage to records, as well as storage facilities and an issuing area, Mac proposed that part of the newsroom be used and that some of the magazines and newspapers be transferred to the reading room. No immediate staff changes were needed but in due course it was likely that two more full-time staff would be required. The rules and regulations were set out for approval by the town clerk and Mac hoped the whole system would be ready for use early in 1955[110]. Through a joint statement with Mac, the town clerk pointed out that, although no mention of gramophone records was made in the 1892 Libraries Act, in 1947 the Minister of Health had defined music as both an art and a science, and a gramophone record was therefore a 'specimen' and as such a legitimate object for a library to store and lend. No charge could be made either per loan or as membership, although some libraries did charge for a catalogue of records held. Payments for damaged records could be used for replacements, but not held over to the following financial year[111].

***

The Roland Hill connection to Bruce Castle made the idea of a philatelic group particularly appropriate. In due course, a society was formed with a children's stamp collectors' section developing within it[112]. The lectures were more ambitious, with nationally known writers talking about their books. An example was A. F. Tschiffely, whose account of his journey from Buenos Aires to Washington DC with two ponies, *Tschiffely's Ride*, was a popular read at the time. By the 1949-50 season, such speakers as Val Gielgud, Vera Brittain and Wynford Vaughan-Thomas were among the presenters.

A scheme to encourage reading was the subject of a report from Mac in March 1950. Normally, books on a given subject were spread throughout the branches and particular titles could be brought to the appropriate branch to meet a request. The special subject displays put on show all the outstanding

---

110 Director's Report Nov 1954
111 Joint statement from Town Clerk and Director December 1954
112 Director's Report July 1949

books on a particular subject in one display, which moved from branch to branch with six weeks in each. Topics such as biographies, non-fiction bestsellers, filmed books and short stories had proved very popular and led to a considerable increase in loans in all branches[113].

***

By the time Mac was working in Tottenham, petrol was available, but still rationed.

"I'm on the look-out for a car," he said to Phyl. "We should be able to get out and about a bit more. It would be easier getting over to Madge and Will and to Maldon, for Keith to have a play in the pool."

"That would be lovely," said Phyl. "Would it be expensive?"

"Oh I'll get something from before the war, there's not much new about yet."

A few weeks later, Phyl was cooking in the kitchen when Mac opened the back door and smiled. "Come and have a look."

"Oh, you've got one. What is it?"

"A Jowett 10 horsepower; it needs a lot of work."

"Can we go for a ride, just up the road I mean, to see what it's like."

At that moment Keith arrived back from school.

"Daddy, Mummy, what's this? Is it ours? Can we have a ride?"

Mac took them on a short ride over to Terling and back and pointed out the uneven note of the engine. Over subsequent weekends he stripped the engine down, sealed a crack in the cylinder head, and put a new gasket in place. He reset the tappets and the timer, and replaced the distributor. Keith was fascinated by the engine parts and asked endless questions as he watched his father working. Mac explained everything with great patience. At last they risked a family outing to Maldon, where they sat in the park and had a picnic while Keith bathed in the paddling pool. When it was time to go they sat in the car and waited while Mac pulled out the choke and pressed the starter button. Nothing happened. Eventually' he told Phyl to take Keith home on the bus while he waited for the carburettor to dry out. In the evening, with Keith in bed, Phyl heard the back door open.

"I had to catch the last bus. I'll have to go back in the morning," said Mac.

"I thought you'd have got it working properly now," said Phyl. "Anyway you'd better have some tea."

---

113 Director's report March 1950

Mac's next task was to strip off the running boards, which were rotting, remake them with plywood and re-cover them with rubber sheeting. Another trip to Maldon was planned. Phyl and Keith sat in the car while Mac locked the kitchen door. He fiddled with his pockets, looked on the floor and then under his seat. "I must have left the car key indoors," he said. "I won't be a minute." Ten minutes later he came out again. "I'm sorry, I can't find it anywhere; all I can think is that I sealed it in the running board. I'm going to have to strip it down again."

Chapter Eleven

Bruce Castle Museum

"There is here a chance for Tottenham to become a pioneer in a valuable experiment in modern display methods." Carnegie Trust letter.

Although the museum at Bruce Castle had remained open throughout the war it had suffered damage, which restricted access and impeded restoration to its proper use. The borough engineer was asked to conduct a survey and report on the work required. In the meantime, Columbia Pictures had thanked staff for their help in research for their film, *Royal Mail*, and Shoreditch Training College had included the museum on its list of places students should visit as part of their training[114]. An early exhibition after the war, displaying material illustrating the overland postal service to India, had attracted a lot of interest. A further donation from Mrs Beatrice Hill, a member of the Rowland Hill family, consisted of paintings, letters and photographs relating to the family[115].

Mac worked closely with the curator Mr C. H. Rock, an able and experienced colleague, to produce a practical policy for the museum. They proposed and the committee agreed that the museum should avoid a vast miscellany of overcrowded objects and focus on one or two themes attractively displayed in a way that would interest schoolchildren and teachers. The themes subsequently agreed were local history, postal history and world history. As there was insufficient space for the long-term development of a museum, the council proposed that Bruce Castle should ultimately become a period museum of the seventeenth and eighteenth centuries and a new purpose-built building should be constructed. In the meantime, items which did not fit with the three themes agreed should be disposed of. The curator was asked to ensure his staff did not cause offence to people who had donated items no longer required. The committee commissioned the borough engineer to report on the work that would be necessary to ensure that the floors and staircases were safe and that the lighting was improved. The committee accepted the report that resulted and asked Mac to apply to the Carnegie Trust for a grant towards the necessary work[116].

In his director's report outlining these issues, Mac had concentrated on the development of the world history theme. Schoolchildren's needs were

---

114 LPBC Min 2101 May 1947
115 LPBC Director's report April 1946
116 LPBC Min Sept 1947

in the forefront of his thinking in the museum, just as they were in the extension activities of the libraries. A history museum should display *'the Woolworths as well as the Bond Street aspect,'* in other words the lives of the poorer classes as well as those of the wealthy. A local school was already using the current history section as a kind of history laboratory, or extra classroom, which the class could use at any time.

In his report for September 1947, Mac wrote:

What is needed, to give life to such a display, is a series of illuminated dioramas illustrating life in various periods, and the conditions that governed societies of different kinds. No existing museum has yet set out to illustrate World History as a single topic, despite the obvious need to spread a 'live' knowledge of history in the world's existing state. There is here a chance for Tottenham to become a pioneer in a valuable experiment in modern display methods.[117]

In January 1948, the curator reported that three refurbished rooms were now open, two for world history and one for local history. Three more were still under repair and preparation. There were eleven or twelve school class visits each month, and teachers were particularly appreciative of the school loans service. There were often as many as six teachers at one time looking for pictures, documents or artefacts to borrow through the system. By April, the curator reported that the loan service was growing so quickly that it could not sustain such increases without more staff and assistance with transport costs. Exhibitions in Manchester and Croydon had made use of postal items, and the BBC was considering which items to include in a television project on postal history.

In response to the request for a grant towards the cost of the plans, two inspectors from the Carnegie Trust made a detailed study of the current exhibitions and the plans for further development. They issued a comprehensive report, which recognised the quality both of the current focus on the three themes and the originality of the plans. They concentrated their attention on the world history exhibition. They praised the way the curator had achieved a balance between the various periods and areas. They were also impressed by the quality and variety of pictures and charts that comprised the current exhibition and fully supported the proposal to add the dioramas displaying key areas. Their one concern was the unsuitability of the rooms. They felt the current rooms were too high, too square and a source of needless expense. A new building was essential in their view. They did support the curator in continuing to develop the exhibition, as

---

117 Director's Report Sept 1947

unique in the country, with a view to relocating it to a new building in due course. They agreed to donate £750 towards the project.[118]

Meanwhile the school loans scheme continued to grow. Demand was particularly high at the beginning of the college teaching practice period. Essex Education Committee had agreed to fund their transport costs but Middlesex were still considering the matter. Duplicates of the most popular loan items were being made, but the scheme was running smoothly most of the time. School loans continued to increase and demand grew for natural history items. These were not on display to the public but, to meet these demands, they were rearranged within the store to improve access for schools. The pressure on staff caused by the school loans had meant that the development of the world history scheme had been rather neglected, but a newly appointed technician was working to overhaul the old exhibits and set up new ones. A re-formed local history group now met regularly at Bruce Castle.[119]

The curator received a significant contribution to the modernisation of the museum in the form of seven dioramas presented to him at The Children's Museum Conference by the Imperial Institute. Some were added to the world history scheme and the others displayed in the children's room[120]. With this increase in content and the accompanying increase in visitors, the curator appealed, through Mac, for the end of the rental agreement with the W. V. S. for the occupation of the ground floor[121]. The space was convenient for new displays and presentations, as well as making it easier to receive and dispatch items.

The repairs of the first floor rooms were completed in early 1950, giving space for the expanding world history section. This attracted positive comments from a range of national and international museum professionals, including those from Turkey and South Africa. A large new notice board outside the entrance also attracted local interest. The recently appointed school services assistant contributed to the setting up of a new room for children to take a more active part in exploring the museum. They were encouraged to gain a more lasting experience from the displays by the provision of quiz sheets and facilities for sketching and model making. A series of filmstrips on the history of Tottenham were also available under the school loans scheme[122].

---

118 Letter from Carnegie Trust with Director's report, July 1948.
119 Curator's report March 1949
120 Director's Report Oct 1949
121 Director's Report Jan 1950
122 Director's Report Oct 1950

All these efforts, but particularly the dioramas conveying the world history scheme, and the curator, Mr Rock, who had set up the exhibition, impressed inspectors from the joint committee of the Carnegie Trust and the Museums Association. They agreed to the grant request and sent congratulations to Mr Rock[123].

At the end of 1950, Mr Rock left to take up a new post. As the new budget required some savings, Mac proposed that the staffing of the museum should be modified so that a senior museums assistant took day-to-day control. Much of the local history and archives would return to the library to manage. He would give more time, in place of the curator, to the overseeing of museum organisation and activities. He suggested this arrangement should be reviewed after a year.

Over the next six months, he brought all the school loan scheme objects together into one room. This led to increased use by Tottenham teachers. He also arranged a clear-out of duplicate and useless objects, thus creating more room for the development of a much larger public display of Tottenham history[124]. The loss of Mr Rock and the staff changes that ensued led to serious staffing problems in the museum. They were perhaps the most urgent in a staffing crisis across the whole of the libraries and museum sector and were highlighted in Mac's report to the committee in November 1953.

The local archives committee had been set up to identify, collect and preserve historical documents relating to the history of Tottenham and register them with the National Register of Archives. The committee included members of the public who had expressed an interest in such work. The director, Mac, was the secretary and the curator the assistant secretary. On Mr Rock's departure, Mac suggested his deputy, Mr A. G. Enser, be appointed to oversee the invitation of members of the public who had shown an interest in joining the committee.

In September 1954, the Postal Collection was enhanced when the general secretary of the Post Office Workers' Union presented an album of Postal Union Commemoration Stamps on behalf of the Union. This became a permanent exhibit in the collection.[125]

Mac subsequently reported on his attendance at the annual conference of the Museums Association. The item that had impressed him was the presentation by Richie Calder, science correspondent of the News Chronicle,

---

123 Letter from chairman, joint committee, Carnegie U.K. Trustees and Museums Association. Oct 1950
124 Director's Report Nov 1951
125 Director's Report Sept 1954

who had emphasised the need to liven up museum displays and make them attractive to 'the man in the street'. Mac gave the practical example of various museums in Edinburgh which had café facilities providing light refreshments. He found these very welcome after a couple of hours browsing the displays and discovered that they were sufficiently popular that they easily covered their costs[126].

***

By 1957, the annual buildings survey had repeatedly drawn attention to the state of one of the semi-octagonal turrets and it was finally agreed to repair it. Once work started, the damage was discovered to be far more extensive than the surveys had suggested, Not only was the brickwork crumbling away but dry rot in the timbers was exposed when previous treatment elsewhere in the building was thought to have dealt with the problem. In May the recommendation of temporary closure for safety while repairs were carried out, was agreed.[127] As a result a number of items now considered unnecessary were disposed of.

In September 1957 the borough engineer wrote to the Ministry of Works quoting the reports of the inspector of ancient monuments and the architect. The inspector, R. Curnow, described Bruce Castle as a 16th century building with two semi-octagonal turrets, one of which had been unavoidably dismantled due to damaging deterioration. It boasted two extremely good 18th century staircases and was confirmed as an ancient monument under the terms of the Act. The architect visited in May and again in August, by which time the first turret had been dismantled. He reported that the building had been well looked after and it should be possible to save the second turret.

In November, the town clerk reported on the reply from the Ministry of Works to his request for a contribution, under the Ancient Monuments Act, towards the £30,000 costs of restoring the building. Predictably there was no money available. The minister suggested approaching the Historic Buildings Council[128].

In January 1958, Mr Chuter Ede MP and a colleague visited on behalf of the Historic Buildings Council. They agreed on the historical and architectural importance of the building and were impressed by the expenditure and work already undertaken by the borough. Mr Chuter Ede pointed out that the

---

126 Director's Report Jan 1955
127 Director's Reports June, July 1957
128 Town Clerk's Report November 1957

association could not make 100% grants but he undertook to recommend a contribution towards the estimated £30,000 costs. There was an intense effort by the committee to obtain a commitment to a specific percentage, but the process would involve the Historical Buildings Association making a recommendation for the Minister of Works to consider. His agreement on the size of the grant would be required before any money could be released. Mr Chuter Ede suggested that the work be spread over three years, in which case a half-penny rate would raise £10,000, leaving the Association to allocate two thirds of the cost. Both parties would return to their councils and update them for discussion.[129]

In the event, the Historic Buildings Association offered only £10,000 but recognised that the borough council could not reasonably raise more than the £10,000 already discussed. They suggested that trusts, such as the Gulbenkian and Carnegie, be approached, as well as leading figures in commerce and industry. The committee themselves added the Post Office and the Postal Workers' Union as other possibilities. All but the Postal Workers' Union turned down the request.

The borough engineer offered four alternatives: full demolition, partial demolition with additional build to house the museum, full restoration, or restoration with additional hall for events and separate entrance and conveniences. The latter was agreed by the council dependant on the agreement and grant from the Historic Buildings Association. In January 1959, the ministry agreed on the £10,000 grant subject to the various anticipated conditions and, in the following month, the town clerk reported that the finance committee had made provision for a £10,000 loan so that work could commence.

In April, an appeal committee was set to prepare for a launch in the September. The town clerk was appointed general secretary and Mac appeals secretary. In July the Postal Workers' Union contributed £2,500.[130] Annual reports detailed the progress towards the target and the borough engineer reported on the progress of the restoration programme. In January 1963, he drew members' attention to the approaching completion of the work and emphasised the need to agree on how the accommodation was to be used: in particular, the suggestion of a public hall on the ground floor and an extension to house the school loans service[131]. By June the following year, the engineer reported that there was still work to complete and that, as the builders would be fully engaged in school works during the summer

129 PLBC chair's report Jan 1958
130 Town Clerk's Reports October 1958 – July 1959.
131 Borough Engineer's report Jan 1963

holidays; it was unlikely that the outstanding work could be completed by the end of March 1965. In addition there was an overspend of approximately £10,000. The town clerk agreed to apply for an additional ministry grant[132].

Meanwhile, in July 1957, Mac had attended the Annual Museums Conference in Bristol, and reported on the discussion on the future responsibility for museums. The government view was that museums and art galleries were essentially a local matter. The Museums Association Council's view was that some form of national funding for the service was vital, but a Regional Museums Service could be a workable compromise.[133]

At the Annual Conference a year later, Mac was entertained by what he described as a 'spirited and witty attack' on the government in support of a resolution deploring its persistently negative attitude to the granting of assistance to local museums and galleries and urging the establishment of a Regional Museum Service, as the previous conference had suggested.[134] The issue was discussed again at the 1959 Conference, when the four key issues were identified: staff qualifications and pay; the standard of conservation work; attention to buildings and display; and realistic and elastic purchase grants[135]. It was not until September 1960, however, that Mac could report that a meeting in St Albans had set up a committee of investigation into all aspects of a Museums and Art Galleries Area Council.[136]

In April 1961, Mac and his chairman attended a meeting as representatives of museum authorities in London, and reported on the agreed proposal that they should be part of a combined South Midlands and South Eastern Federations Area Council and, that London museums should form one of a number of sub-areas[137]. In January 1963, Mac and the town clerk presented a copy of a draft document on these issues for the committee's consideration. The main concern was the means of financing it. The suggestion of ten shillings per thousand population of the authority concerned was complicated by the inclusion of local borough councils within county councils, and thus the potential for double payments. The ongoing discussions concerning the creation of the Greater London Council were an added complication[138].

A month later, Mac was able to report that the proposals had now been

132 Borough Engineer's report June 1964
133 Director's Report October 1957
134 Director's Report Oct 1958
135 Director's Report July 1959
136 Director's Report Sept 1960
137 Director's Report Feb 1961
138 Town Clerk & Director's Report Jun 1963

amended to resolve the financial issues and, at the June 1963 meeting of the committee, Mac presented the revised constitution of the Area Museums and Art Galleries Council. His recommendation to join was accepted and their chairman was nominated as their representative[139]. A year later Mac reported on the annual meeting of the council and was clearly frustrated that, although he was their authorised representative standing in for their chairman, an earlier amendment precluding officers from voting denied him a vote in the proceedings.[140]

***

In celebration of the twenty-fifth anniversary of the Charter in 1959, a number of sound recordings of the memories of older residents of the borough were made and edited. These were played as part of an evening function, 'The Old Days', which was very well attended. This led to further stories and photographs being offered and added to the local history collection. Mac sought permission to record more memories of older residents and of eminent residents associated with contemporary events in the borough. These would then be preserved permanently in the local history collection.[141] In response to requests from a number of committee members, Mac arranged for some examples to be played at the end of the September meeting.

139 Town Clerk & Director's Report Jun 1963
140 Director's Report June 1964
141 Director's Report July 1959

Chapter Twelve

Under Pressure

"Many members of staff have reason to remember your help and kindness to them."

The early nineteen fifties saw some major changes in Mac's family life. As he was driving along the A414 near Hemel Hempstead, on the return journey from their holiday in Wales after the broadcast, the Jowett had chugged loudly to a standstill as the exhaust pipe had rusted through. Mac had carried out a temporary repair by breaking off the small tin door on the biscuit box he had converted into a container for the primus stove during the war. He now took the stove on holiday so that he could brew a cup of tea during a break in the journey. He had been impressed by the new green Morris Oxford of Leslie Thomas, the Swansea bookseller friend they had spent time with on the recent holiday. He was able to buy a very similar, but less powerful, Morris Cowley and dispense with the Jowett.

A much more serious and more stressful change involved Keith's education.

"I think he should go to Brentwood School," he said to Phyl. "It is much the best school in the area. It will guarantee him the best education we can give him."

"But it's a long way for a little boy to travel every day and it's expensive, isn't it? I mean, I know David went there but Madge lives in the area; it was his local grammar school."

"He'll pass the scholarship; we know his intelligence is there from the tests at the Educational Research Centre and he's always top or nearly top at school. He'll just have to pass the entrance exam and he'll be in."

"It's expecting a lot; he won't have any friends there, and then there's the travel every day."

"Well, I was thinking we could move to the area. He'd make new friends there, I'd be nearer work and you'd be near to Madge and Will. Anyway, it's time we bought our own house," said Mac.

"Have you been thinking this all along? This is the first time you've mentioned it."

"I've said about Brentwood School before, and we have always wanted to buy our own house."

"Well, I must admit it sounds attractive, but it puts an awful lot of pressure on Keith."

Mac found a vacant plot of land in Priests Lane in Shenfield. It was a few minutes from Shenfield Station, from where the electric trains ran into Liverpool Street, and it was only about a mile from Brentwood School. During 1951, he worked with a local architect from Brentwood to design a chalet bungalow, and the plans were presented to him in January 1952. Negotiations continued throughout the early months and the contract was signed on 24th July 1952. By this time Keith had passed the eleven-plus and the entrance exam for Brentwood School and was due to start there in September. The house was due to be completed by 20th December but completion was delayed until the following April. This had worried Phyl as Keith, still only eleven years old, had to catch a train at Hatfield Peverel station at 7.25 am and did not get home until 5.45 pm. For much of the period he travelled in darkness. They finally moved in during the Easter holidays.

Mac now had his own dedicated study. He could look out, through Crittall's finest metal-framed windows across the wasteland behind the house and plan a wonderful garden. In his mind he would now have some leisure time to create it. Phyl had always pottered around in the garden at Hatfield Peverel, so once he had mapped out the grand sweep of the land, the long oval lawns, the colourful, curvaceous flower beds, the ornamental pond, perhaps with soothing spring-like fountain … so his thoughts would run on. Phyl would be glad to work at the detail, the hoeing, weeding, dead-heading and so on. Keith was getting bigger too; no doubt he would give a hand with the heavier tasks.

The room was light and bright, with pale green emulsioned walls, white woodwork and a small white radiator, offering a gesture towards central heating. His beechwood office chair was a disappointingly modern utility, as were the fitted bookshelves, yet they provided a light contrast against the dark mahogany and the navy and brown bindings on many of the books. The carpet also had a light green pattern and the plain door through to the hall matched the beechwood shelves.

He would sit at his dark mahogany desk, with its carved, cloven-hoofed legs, elegant brass-handled drawers and inset leather top, stained by generations of mugs and tankards offering refreshment and distraction. Pen nibs, staplers and other stationery impedimenta had pitted the surface in irregular and arbitrary shapes towards the right-hand side. The General

Post Office issue telephone and local telephone directory stood on the corner of the desk. In the wide, shallow, central drawer he kept his geometrical instruments: the usual compass and dividers, together with a large 180° angle protractor and 30° and 45° set squares. These he would use to plan and sketch the garden layout but, together with his treasured slide rule, he would also use them for diagrams as he developed his theories of reading needs and book stock logistics, which were at the core of his contribution to the development of the role of public libraries.

In spite of the pleasures of house and garden, it was for his library work that he valued his study the most. The shelves along the wall behind him were proof of this. The books they housed ranged from philosophical studies, psychology, and critical thinking to mathematics, science and the scientific attitude. The fundamental concepts therein were mastered and applied as further volumes were added on human communication, literary criticism and bibliographical studies. Another area of the shelves contained his growing collection of early editions of the classics, including a signed copy of *A Book about Books*, by Robert Blatchford, one of the key players in the development of socialism and the Labour Party before the First World War.

In the mahogany bureau opposite were files and papers, drafts for talks and presentations which were the result of all this study. In the bottom drawer, as well as family memorabilia, he kept, carefully wrapped in soft yellow dusters, two white stone statuettes showing Marx and Lenin in contemplative mood; a fact that put Phyl in fear of his sudden arrest should they ever be discovered.

***

Once they had moved to Shenfield life became much easier, although Phyl made no more that a polite acquaintance with neighbours and relations with her sister Madge seemed inexplicably frosty. With his new, more reliable car and shorter distance to work, Mac no longer spent committee nights with his parents. His father had retired in 1952, after working as a salesman for Truman's Beers since 1934. Shortly afterwards, Mac's parents moved to a bungalow in Thundersley in Essex. Mac and Phyl were visiting them in April 1958 when Mac noticed that his father's cigarette had burned down to the stub in his hand without him raising it to inhale. Alarmed, he spoke and then stood and touched his father. It was clear that he was dead. After the immediate reaction, and looking after his shocked and devastated mother, Mac had the job of managing the funeral, the will, and his mother's

104

care. He eventually moved her to a flat a short distance from his house in Shenfield where she lived until she died in 1967.

***

In October 1951 the Conservatives, led by Winston Churchill, won a narrow victory in the general election. Mac was disappointed but not surprised. Most people were fed up with the post-war austerity and looked forward to the changes that the Conservatives promised. In due course the Chancellor of the Exchequer, Rab Butler, cut income tax and purchase tax and restricted government spending. This inevitably led to problems and delays in pursuing the improvements Mac felt were urgently needed.

Perhaps the most important issue was that of staff pay. The deputy director, Mr A. G. Enser, requested that his salary be regraded to two thirds of the director's salary in line with other chief officers' deputies. The Establishment Sub-Committee ruled that the salary relationship did not apply in the case of the Director of Libraries and Museum, but that the Libraries and Public Buildings Committee were free to consider the matter on other grounds[142]. The following month, Mac presented the committee with a breakdown of how the deputy salaries related to that of their chief librarians in almost all the London boroughs. The overall average was 65%[143]. The problems were wider ranging, and causing Mac increasing concern. The deputy director continued to put pressure on Mac in spite of the comprehensive and detailed case Mac had made to the committee. Mac was broadly sympathetic, but was increasingly concerned about the wider issue of low pay and its impact on the service. The discussion over the re-grading of the deputy director's pay and the removal of the post of curator of Bruce Castle Museum from the establishment were symptoms of serious problems which had developed with staffing. In November 1953, Mac presented a detailed report of the current responsibilities and organisation of the department, followed by the various contributory factors to the difficulties the department now faced and the implications for the service they were designed to provide.

He listed five main areas of activity: the library service at central, four branches and the mobile service; the management of four public halls; Bruce Castle Museum; the schools service; and the bindery and printing section. Members of staff were employed as agreed under the *Service in Depth* system, with administration and professional roles distinct where

---

142 Director's report Dec 1952
143 Director's report Jan 1953

105

possible. Since the current establishment had been agreed, the law had reduced working hours from 39 to 38, and increased holidays. In addition, in-service training had increased as had sickness leave. The success of various initiatives had also increased demand.

The problem was most acute in the general administration section, where resignations had led to a 100% turnover and the struggle to recruit had been costly and time-consuming. The additional pressure of the extra workload, the requirement for evening work and the half day not matching friends in other jobs, in addition to the comparatively low pay and lack of an intermediate salary grade, all contributed to low recruitment levels. The only route to higher pay was through a stiff examination programme. In short, it was easy enough for school leavers to get more highly paid work with more attractive working conditions. The impact of all these problems was the equivalent of being permanently short of nine posts, and the lack of a curator for the museum was a matter demanding immediate attention.

***

The build-up of these various pressures affected Mac's health. Phyl would bathe a series of painful boils which developed on his neck. Keith was also prone to boils as he entered adolescence and they would sit together in the kitchen while Phyl bathed first her husband's and then her son's painful necks. The pressures became so great that, early in 1955, Mac had a nervous breakdown. He lay in bed tossing and turning, occasionally crying out or weeping into his pillow. The breakdown lasted several weeks and he missed one monthly committee meeting. Phyl blamed the pressure Pat Enser had put on him over his salary, but later Mac made clear that the impact of the wages issue on staff recruitment and stability, combined with building delays and Bruce Castle Museum issues overwhelmed him as they threatened to destroy the continuation of the *Service in Depth* system that had offered such promise. By the summer he had recovered sufficiently to return to work.

***

In October 1957, the council of the London and Home Counties Library Association issued a report on the difficulties of recruitment and retention of public library staff as detailed in a survey on the year to December 1956. There was a loss on average of 20% of staff, and the recruitment of a very low number of male staff. The main reasons were low pay and prospects, awkward hours and Saturday working. As salaries were not competitive, the jobs had developed a reputation as transit camps until opportunities arose to move on. The report provided a detailed analysis and proposed measures in addition to recommending a general rise in salaries.

The report pointed out that professional qualifications should be linked with a financial reward to guarantee an immediate pay rise on qualification. In addition there should be special recognition for someone who achieves a final qualification as opposed to an intermediate one. The report concluded by questioning whether local government could continue to deliver quality local services while paying such uncompetitive salaries[144].

Part of the problem, as the town clerk reported, was that all newly appointed trainees were awarded the same basic starting salary, regardless of age and qualification. The current candidates, for example, varied between an unqualified young man of 15 years 9 months and an 18-year-old, with five G.C.E 'O' levels, and two 'A' levels. The Establishment Sub-Committee had been considering the introduction of scales based on age and qualification and sought the support of the Middlesex District Whitley Council. That council, in turn, had been considering the implications of such salary scales for the London District Council and for constituent authorities in Middlesex. Their decision was deferred until the outcome of these consultations was known. The town clerk ended his report by pointing out that it was unlikely that suitable appointments would be made due to the low salaries and urging the Establishment Sub-Committee to give immediate attention to the matter.[145]

In July 1958, Mac informed the committee that A. G. Enser had resigned as deputy director from 1st September 1958[146] to take the post of chief librarian in Eastbourne. At the October meeting Walter Preston was appointed acting deputy until the new appointment was made.[147]

In January 1958, the NALGO representative requested the retrospective re-grading for the printing and binding officer and the binding overseer, in line with the recent staff review. In the same month a circular was received from the Ministry of Housing and Local Government. This referred to the need to strengthen the pound by limiting public expenditure as much as possible. In particular, it stressed the need for local authorities to reduce spending and to avoid any additional spending on salaries without making the savings necessary to minimise the extra expenditure.

---

144 Director's Report October 1957
145 Town Clerk's Report Aug 1957
146 Director's Report July 1958
147 Director's Report Oct 1958

Another frustrating issue during this period was the outdated and inconvenient state of the library buildings. In his February 1950 report, Mac expressed his increasing concern about the inadequacy of the central library building and the branches. He pointed out that the need for rebuilding had been acknowledged before the war. His report considered maintenance, which included minor repairs and redecoration. He was also concerned about accommodation. The need for improving or replacing current accommodation was now acute. The Coombes Croft Branch had been moved to the disused St John's Church in 1940. The building had since become damp throughout and did not have enough basic accommodation. Other branches had varying levels of deterioration, but accommodation was a problem for them all. In most cases, there was not enough storage for reserve stock, and the children's sections were a problem in several branches. It was agreed that Mac would work with the borough engineer to produce a report on the current condition and suggested next steps.

As a result, the St John's building was closed and the adjoining Coombes Croft building was deemed to need major work. In June 1954, the borough engineer and surveyor responded to a request to modify the central library extension scheme so that it could be carried out in two stages. Stage one would involve building the front part of the extension only and retaining the temporary building, currently the lending library, as the rear portion of the scheme. Stage two would involve replacing the temporary structure with the other section of the extension. In January 1955, a new survey recommended delaying central library issues until agreed new work commenced the following year. In September 1956 the extension work was further delayed.

Totally frustrated, Mac now prepared comprehensive plans for urgent improvements, especially of working conditions for staff. These included, increased lavatory provision, a rest room for women, and improved staff room provision in the light of meals having to be taken there. He also wanted lockers for staff in rooms rather than corridors and a reduction of service points to be manned in the evening.

Mac proposed that the central hall should be taken over for providing the extra space and that a panel wall cutting off the children's library should be taken down. The larger area of the library that this created should be closed half an hour early so that some meetings could be held there; others could be transferred to other branch library halls. In addition, he proposed various minor modifications to the first floor and ground floor layouts. All these measures were essential for staff morale. The borough engineer had recommended a complete rewiring of the system. In addition, more storage facilities were required, as was the redecoration which had been repeatedly deferred.

By July 1957, further deferment to the extension programme led to the company appointed to arrange for the submission of tenders putting in a claim for £2,200 to cover the cost as no tenders were taken up. Some improvement work in the central library did take place in the second half of the year and further works were found to be necessary as a result. At the end of the year, central government imposed severe restrictions on public building expenditure, delaying further improvements. Only in 1962 did the second stage of improvements to the central library begin, and in the following year the third stage was approved for the financial year 1964-5.

***

Mac continued to be concerned about Keith's education. His son had not done as well as he had hoped. Keith had done well in the school scout troop. He had travelled widely across Europe on camping trips, and this had freed Mac and Phyl to take holidays in Germany, Austria and Switzerland. A number of these were study tours where Mac explored the library systems involved, explained his *Service in Depth* system and invited a number of his hosts to visit Tottenham. Academically, Keith did well enough at 'O' levels but clearly had not conformed to school discipline in other ways. He was allowed entry to the sixth form, but his subject choice was limited. He obtained provisional places at two universities but did not achieve the required grades. In the summer of 1959 Keith was casting around for temporary jobs. Mac was deeply disappointed as his son took a job as a petrol pump attendant at a local garage. A week later, through a chance meeting with one of his teachers who lived nearby, Keith was encouraged to apply to St David's College, Lampeter. His teacher assured him that his exam results were good enough to gain him a place there. His application was successful so, much to Mac's relief, Keith would have a university education after all. Mac was also pleased the following summer, when Keith took a temporary job as a relief at Brentwood Library. He was intrigued by the car Keith arrived home in, a 1936 Armstong-Siddeley, which he had bought by paying the garage bill for a friend who could not afford it. One day, when Keith was ready for work, the car wouldn't start. He managed to catch a bus and arrive in time but was astonished, as the end of his shift approached, to see his car parked outside. He immediately offered a lift home to the very attractive library assistant who had responded positively to his interest. She was as impressed as he had hoped with the car and, after an affectionate farewell; Keith drove home in high spirits. His father arrived home half an hour later.

"Where did you get to with the car?" said Mac.

"I took a friend home and then came home myself."

"I was only gone a few minutes. I popped round to the shops and when I came back the car had gone. I spent all morning and half the afternoon, sorting it out. Then I came to fetch you and you'd left me to get home on my own."

"I'm sorry, Dad. I thought you'd brought it over for me and gone home."

Keith obtained a good honours degree and went on to qualify as a teacher. Mac's relief was short-lived, however, as Keith's first year in teaching did not go well. Mac restrained himself with difficulty from visiting and berating the head teacher. After a change of school, however, Keith made the most of his second chance, married a very attractive girl and finally seemed to settle down.

Chapter Thirteen

Local Government Reorganisation

"There is little I need say about the quite remarkable staff spirit which has persisted for so long at Tottenham; it has been greater than any newcomer, or I imagine, Chief, dare hope for."

In October 1955, a memorandum from the council of the Library Association was presented for approval. It laid out the duties under the 1892 Public Libraries Act, and detailed the risks to the service in the reorganisation of local government. In particular, the proposed transfer of all public library services into the relevant county service was likely to reduce some well-run services in cities and boroughs. Financial provision varied greatly from authority to authority, but many had rateable values well below the level required to maintain an effective service that met its statutory duties.

The memorandum proposed that suitable library authorities be created by the surrender to county library services of all library authorities with a rateable value in 1953/4 of less than £300,000, or that joint services be provided; that each authority should appoint a library committee responsible only for library matters; that the system should ensure financial provision for an adequate library service; and that a government department should be established to ensure financial provision and improving standards of provision.

In the context of a general reform of local government in England and Wales, the Minister of Education set up, in September 1957, a committee, under the chairmanship of Sir Sydney Roberts, *'to consider the structure of the public library service in England and Wales, and to advise what changes, if any, should be made in the administrative arrangements, regard being had to the relation of public libraries to other libraries'*. The report of this committee was published in February 1959.

***

At the April committee meeting at Tottenham, Mac included a letter from the secretary of the Non-county Boroughs Committee, which contained a resolution strongly opposing the proposed transfer of library services from boroughs to county councils and asking the Association of Municipal Councils to do all in its power to prevent the implementation of this policy. The letter went on to suggest a series of other measures to oppose this element of the report.

With the committee's agreement, Mac deferred discussion until he had had time to study the report in detail. The following month he gave an in-depth report on his recommended response. Typically, he had taken a step back from the instant reaction. As he said, at first sight it seemed as if an attack on non-county libraries, however effective they were, was the driving force behind the report. Yet it was important to keep in mind the purpose of the report and its terms of reference, which involved examining the structure of the public library system and advising what changes, if any, should be made to its administrative arrangements.

The committee looked at the functions of the public library as agreed in the report of a previous committee in 1927; functions which Mac had rehearsed in his centenary broadcast back in 1950. It was all too easy to see the service as simply a provision of light entertainment. Fundamentally the public library was an essential service, of national importance for intellectual study and free access to knowledge, ideas and opinion. It followed that minimum standards of service should be set nationally, but administered locally. National administration could lead to censorship and restrictions which would defeat the purpose and function of the service. Therefore, Mac said, the minister should be obliged to allow any local authority deemed to meet the agreed standards to continue to run the service[148].

The Minister of Education was duly given general responsibility for overseeing minimum standards for the service, but two further committees were set up to look in more detail at aspects of the report before any legislation was considered. The first of these, chaired by H. T. Bourdillon, carried out a detailed study of up-to-date library practice and made a series of recommendations on standards of staffing and premises, lending and reference sections and children's services, as well as support for adult cultural and educational activities. The other committee, chaired by E. B. H. Baker, reported on inter-library co-operation.

In January 1963, Mac reported on the proposals from these committees drawn up in preparation for the Public Libraries and Museums Bill. Mac had been able to compare Tottenham to the results in a number of categories in the tables used in the first report but had not had time to consider the second as yet. In most categories Tottenham was below the median but on the proportion of lending stock on loan at any one time they were well in front of the highest in the study. Mac agreed to report more fully at a later

---

meeting[149].

Meanwhile, in January 1961, the town clerk received a letter from the Ministry of Housing and Local Government, asking councils to comment on key issues raised in its report on the reform of local government in the London area. In particular, it sought views on the proposal that new boroughs should be formed with populations between 100,000 and 250,000. The boroughs should be the authorities responsible for all but a short list of functions that would clearly be better managed across a wider area. A directly elected council for Greater London should be responsible for such issues as planning, traffic management and highways, education, personal health and ambulance services. All views submitted would be circulated and discussed by ministers and departments. Seventeen copies were required.

In response, Mac submitted a series of observations to the Public Libraries and Museum Committee. He suggested that a larger local authority would mean savings in general administration, book-binding and, if the printing section could be enlarged to take in the increased requirements, the unit cost would come down and more flexibility would be possible. Larger book stocks, more professional staff and reduced inter-lending between authorities would also bring an improved service and reduce costs.

Mac thought it very important that schools and library services should be the responsibility of the same authority, which should be the borough. He also suggested the inter-lending scheme should be within the new Greater London Area and should continue on the current co-operative basis between librarians.

The committee adopted all these suggestions which were then forwarded to the Ministry.[150]

***

At the same time there were two attempts to introduce a Public Lending Right. This would require public libraries to pay a charge of one penny for every loan above two thousand in a year of any particular book. One Bill put before parliament had a second reading before being talked out. Mac and the town clerk presented the committee with a paper listing many problems such a charge would cause. Among these was the estimate that the administrative cost to libraries would equal the amount paid out. Thus the council would have to find an estimated extra £4,500 or reduce the number of books purchased. The proposal did not distinguish between loans of

149 Director's Report Jan 1963
150 Director's report and Minister's letter January 1961

children's books, scientific or technical works and recreational reading. The paper listed a number of further issues before a reiteration of Mac's strong belief expressed in the final paragraph:

'It cannot be overstressed that the Public Library Service is now the only universal means available for the distribution of ideas and attitudes freely throughout the community and which is not subject to powerful or monopolistic interest. Any additional financial burdens upon it will inevitably impair its efficacy for educational and democratic development.' [151]

Although committee members feared further attempts to introduce such a charge, it was not until 1979 that the Public Lending Right Act became law. This did not charge library authorities, but used a sampling method to calculate payments which were then made from a central fund.

***

In April 1964, the elections were held for the new boroughs in the Greater London Council. As a result Haringey Borough Council, combining Tottenham with Wood Green and Hornsey, was inaugurated and formed its committees. The Library, Museum and Arts Committee met and decided to interview the three directors for the post of borough librarian for the new borough.

As the interview day approached, Mac was increasingly worried about the outcome.

"With Herbert away the Tottenham members could well be outvoted," he said.

"But surely," said Phyl, "they'll have to pick you? Tottenham is the biggest authority, isn't it? You've got the museum, and you're well known all over the country for what you've done."

"There's a big emphasis on art activities in Hornsey, that could cause problems, and it's likely they'll all go for their own man."

"But Dougie Clarke is chairing it. He'll give you full backing."

"I'm sure he will, but he has a tendency to over-do it. It puts people's backs up."

"Surely they're not so petty. I'm sure you will be O.K. Good luck, anyway, and drive carefully."

"I'll ring you from Philip's and let you know."

---

151 Town Clerk and Director's Report Feb 1962

At the meeting, Councillor Clarke welcomed each of the three candidates in turn. He gave Mac an encouraging smile, but questions from Wood Green and Hornsey councillors centred on the Service in Depth and on the unconventional layout and shelving at Tottenham. Their staffs were used to operating the accepted systems.

"Would there be a complete reorganisation of their libraries?" said one.

"We will work towards a gradual integration," said Mac. "They will welcome the benefits it brings, both to their work and to borrowers. That's certainly been the experience at Tottenham."

"It's an excellent scheme. It has the Tottenham committee's full support. I can assure councillors it is the right way to go," said Councillor Clarke.

"Yes, thank you, Chairman. We are here to decide that for ourselves. May I suggest that we discuss this without candidates being present?" said another councillor.

"Very well; if there are no more questions for Mr McClellan? No? Thank you Mac. We'll keep you informed."

Mac thanked the panel and left, feeling very uneasy.

When the decision had been made, Councillor Clarke summoned each candidate in turn.

"Mr McClellan," he began. "Thank you for your detailed and impressive responses to our questions." He looked Mac directly in the eyes, frowned and continued, "Unfortunately the panel have decided, having given careful consideration to all the candidates, to offer the post of borough librarian to Mr Stevenson. I am very sorry, Mac," he added.

Mac sat for a full minute. Then stood, mouthed "Thank you," and left the room. He leaned against the wall for a moment. He shook hands with Mr Stevenson and left the building.

A few minutes later, Philip Colehan heard a knock on his front door. He was expecting Mac, as they had arranged that he would call in and ring Phyl to tell her how the interviews had gone. Philip opened the door to see Mac standing there, dumbfounded and white-faced.

"Mac?"

"I didn't get it. They gave it to Stevenson. They gave it to Stevenson, Philip."

"That's crazy! How could they do that? Come in, come in and have a cup of tea, and a brandy if you want, and tell me what happened."

"Most of them seemed to view our system as some kind of way-out experiment. Duggie was very supportive, of course, but they obviously felt he should be neutral as chairman."

"Sounds like he overdid it as usual. I know his heart is in the right place, but … well you know what I mean. Anyway, you'd better ring Phyl. I'll get you that cup of tea."

Somehow Mac managed to drive home. He felt utterly frustrated at the lack of understanding of how Tottenham was meeting the needs of its readers, and at the sudden loss of any way forward for the opportunity to continue to develop his ideas. He was subsequently appointed associate director, to work with the director to draw up the draft establishment of the rest of the department. In October the Library, Museum and Arts Committee formally confirmed the Establishment Committee's recommendation that Mac be appointed as associate director in a supernumerary post, personal to him.[152]

Sadly the system at Tottenham, still known as the Tottenham Experiment at the time, was thus considered of limited application when the other two boroughs had libraries organised on traditional lines. Only in Eastbourne, where Pat Enser, with guidance from Mac, introduced a modified version for his single town library and in Hillingdon, where Philip Colehan was appointed director in November 1964, did the scheme continue with modifications to suit local circumstances.

***

In the midst of all the emotional distress and frustration these events caused, his son added to Mac's turmoil by a sudden courtship and marriage. Mac thought that, with his second chance at Burnt Mill Comprehensive School, where the head teacher had shown sympathy and understanding and offered a new start, Keith would finally settle down. When Keith came home with a very attractive young woman at the weekend of the end of the first month at his new school, Mac was pleased to meet her, and saw it as a sign of Keith's settling in well. When, scarcely a month later, he rang to say they were engaged and planned to marry before the end of the Christmas holiday, he was rather taken aback.

"He can't marry that lovely young girl," said Phyl.

"It is a bit sudden, I agree," said Mac. "But she seems very nice."

"You always had an eye for a pretty girl; that doesn't mean she's suitable. How can he be sure; he's only known her about six weeks? You don't think she's expecting or something?"

---

152 Haringey Library Museum and Art Committee Oct 1964

"Well, if she is, he's doing the right thing by her and, if not, no doubt she soon will be. It would be nice to have a grandchild, wouldn't it? Anyway, I offered to take the photographs. I thought it would be something pleasant to do after all the stress at work," said Mac.

"Are you sure? Don't they usually employ professionals for weddings?"

"They seem happy about it."

The wedding went off well, although the photographs did not. The couple were left with very few pictures of their happy day. They spent their three-day honeymoon in a bed and breakfast near Redcar that Mac had recommended, and returned to work as husband and wife. Phyl's fears about the reason for the sudden marriage were not realised. It was not until June the following year that the imminent arrival of a grandchild became obvious. Mac and Phyl had joined the couple for a tea to celebrate their daughter-in-law, Carol's, birthday. After the meal Carol disappeared briefly and then called Keith. He returned pale-faced and asked his mother to go to his wife. Phyl emerged with a smile. "Her waters have broken. You need to get her to the hospital right away." Their grand-daughter was born in the early hours of the following morning.

***

Towards the end of February 1965, Mac addressed the final meeting of the library committee of Tottenham.

"I should like to record a few comments by way of an epilogue," he said.

"The local authority in Tottenham has at this date operated a library service continuously since 1892, that is, for a period of 73 years. In that time, three librarians have been responsible for its administration: Mr Frederick J. West, Mr Walter J. Bennett and myself. Both Mr West and Mr Bennett founded and built upon a tradition of service to every section of the people of this town and I have continued in this same tradition. It has always been a progressive and in many respects a pioneering service. Many thousands of our people have derived pleasure, enlightenment and inspiration from its activities.

Throughout my period of office, I have been very conscious of the support and confidence I have enjoyed from the libraries committee and its chairman. It has been a great pleasure to work with you and the council and I am deeply grateful.

The key, however, to the running of a successful and appreciated service lies with its staff and employees. In this respect you and I have been singularly fortunate. The essence or philosophy of the public library idea has always seemed to me to consist in offering the opportunity of genuine freedom for the individual to grow in whatever way he feels the need to grow. The sense of responsibility and self-discipline necessary for living and working with others comes naturally when people are free of pressures and the obligation to conform. It is this philosophy which we have tried to embody in our working life within the library. There is a sense of comradeship in your staff and an inherent 'esprit de corps' which have developed over the years and which they themselves have called 'T. P. L. lifemanship.' To have worked with them has been a privilege and a source of pride. In particular, I must pay tribute to my great friend and colleague, Walter Preston. The last few months have been the most trying in my whole career and his loyalty and support during this time have been invaluable."

He finished by adding, "We in the library service take our leave of a great era under Tottenham, with sadness, but we go into Haringey knowing that we have a worthy contribution to bring to it and determined to play our part in forging a new and greater library service."

***

The reaction of the staff at Tottenham is best summed up by a letter Mac received from one of the staff who had left working for Haringey after two years of the new borough.

There is little I need say about the quite remarkable staff spirit which has persisted for so long at Tottenham; it has been greater than any newcomer, or I imagine, Chief, dare hope for. … I shall remember my years at Tottenham for the experience of working in a professional atmosphere in which the courage to experiment and to implement radical theories had triumphed over tradition and conservatism. It may well be that the true achievement at Tottenham will not be apparent for some time yet. The alacrity with which the application of the theories has been attacked suggests that fundamental issues are being grappled with.

Finally I would like to thank you for many personal kindnesses and for many stimulating discussions.

Mac was very moved by this letter and replied in open and revealing terms.

He wrote, in part:

From the time I first appreciated the deeper significance of libraries in our society I wanted to inspire… this same significance among my colleagues working in the library. It seemed to me that the library stood for so much, that those who worked in it should, consciously or unconsciously, absorb into their personal working relationships that same spirit, if they were to be effective. In some instances I think we succeeded in doing this in Tottenham and your remarks are welcome confirmation that it was so.

He continued with a very personal reflection

I think my approach to librarianship might have found readier acceptance if I had gone into teaching and research, although I do not think that I am a good teacher. At this stage of my career, after 40 years service, I feel disappointment that the opportunity for further research appears so limited for me. There is so much to be done and so much to be written about it. Nevertheless, I feel the necessity for a more penetrating understanding of the purpose of libraries and a more scientific attitude of mind in implanting that purpose will find acceptance in due course, and if it does I think I shall have helped to make it more possible.[153]

This proved to be unduly pessimistic about his opportunities for research and writing, but in the immediate future he was asked to transfer from his associate librarian post to carry out some research as assistant town clerk. His travel allowance was transferred accordingly. In his new role, Mac produced a detailed report on *'Currently Discussed Concepts relating to the Administrative Structure of Local Authorities.'* The paper he presented explored local government administrations in America and Ireland as well as in Newcastle-upon-Tyne and Basildon, and made recommendations based on the results. His general comment on presenting the report had, consciously or unconsciously, an ironic touch.

I have resisted the temptation to apologise for the length of the report, he wrote, *because if an adequate background to the discussion was to be available, it was necessary, not only to gather together in one conspectus the most important currents of thinking on the internal organisation of the local authority but that each should be represented … to an extent adequate for understanding. I hope this has been achieved.*[154]

As the new libraries museum and arts organisation began to operate, Mr Stevenson, now the director, refused to work from the office in Bruce Castle <u>which had been</u> designated as the new library service headquarters. By

153 Exchange of letters, April 1966.
154 Report to Functions and Communications Panel Apr 1966

September 1966, Mr Stevenson, and the assistant director, Mr Woodham, had applied for retirement and the ever-loyal Walter Preston was appointed as temporary assistant librarian[155], and subsequently as acting librarian.

With retirement age approaching, Mac and Phyl moved to Ardleigh, near Colchester. Mac developed a skin problem. His skin became very flaky and allergic to light. He spent a short period in hospital where he had his arms and legs wrapped in bandages for protection. And later a light test was arranged. He was able to retire after his sixtieth birthday in May 1968. A formal farewell was held at the Civic Centre, but as another former staff member wrote to him:

I would far rather remember the more informal do we had at the [Bruce] castle with the library set.

I would like to thank you for those years at Tottenham when your infectious keenness made the work so interesting and worthwhile to us all. I particularly remember how the staff worked as a team and a request for an interview whether for business or personal reasons always met with a ready response. Many members of staff have reason to remember your help and kindness to them – not least myself.

With this and many other such messages, Mac and Phyl settled down to a quiet life in their new house in Ardleigh. It did not remain quiet for long.

---

155 Libraries Museums and Arts Report September 1966

Chapter Fourteen

New Opportunities

"Your father's collection is a magnificent augmentation of the Library's resources, most especially because of the materials in his files."

Early in January 1968, Keith and his family flew out to live and work in Kenya. Over the next six years, Keith wrote weekly letters describing their life there. He also sent regular photos and films from his super-8 cine camera. They were living in Yala, a remote village in the far west of the country. The letters and photos caused Phyl, in particular, endless worry. They seemed to be ill very often and their little daughter, Lisa, looked thin and bedraggled in the early photos. More worrying was the knowledge that Carol was pregnant. How on earth would she cope with childbirth so far from hospital? What sort of care would a tiny baby get? If the photos of Lisa were anything to go by, God help the little treasure. She missed her granddaughter terribly, and now another grandchild was on the way and she may never see him or her.

At the same time, Arch's skin problem flared again and he was back in hospital in February. The problem was quickly resolved, however, and he returned to work, travelling up to Tottenham by train every day. He was advised to keep out of the sun to avoid any further problems and bought himself an astrakhan hat, much to Phyl's amazement; he could never bear anything touching his head. As his sixty-first birthday approached at the end of May he looked forward to his retirement, but at the same time he applied for the post of Parish Clerk in Ardleigh. He was interviewed and appointed from 1st of July.

Once Mac was established in his new role, he and Phyl developed a strong friendship with the parish council chairman, Garth Simmonds and his wife, Peggy. Now Mac was involved in the local community, Phyl began to join in activities and make friends in a way she had not done since they moved away from Tottenham. Mac was appreciated for his interest in the lives and well-being of the parishioners and for the warm welcome visitors received when they visited the delightful new home Mac and Phyl had created.

In August they had a letter from Keith in Yala, informing them that they now had a grandson. Phyl was both thrilled and fearful and was not impressed by the name, Lee. She used his second name, Rory, when she thought about him. Mac tried to reassure her and felt they should accept

Keith and Carol's choice of names, even if they were what Phyl thought of as a bit common.

"We're behind the times, Phyl," he said. "They're only keeping up to date; it's the sixties."

"Poor kid'll regret it when he's older," said Phyl. "Still he looks a little sweetie in the photo." Both grandchildren's health continued to be a worry to her and she missed regular contact with them terribly.

***

As Mac had written in the letter to his colleague, *I feel disappointment that the opportunity for further research appears so limited for me. There is so much to be done and so much to be written about it.* He still hankered after the continuing opportunity to be involved in some way in the theory of libraries and librarianship. His enthusiasm was clear when he gave advice to a young friend of Keith's and also to a nephew, both of whom were considering a career in librarianship. A young librarian in Brentwood described Mac's writings as a breath of fresh air after the dull text books on the course, and an academic from UL described him as the foremost thinker in libraries since the war. In November, he was invited to present a paper at a conference in Edinburgh. This was very well received and, in April 1969, he gave a lecture at the College of Librarianship in Aberystwyth. Mac was impressed with the college and its setting in an attractive mountainous area a few miles from a spectacular coastline. He also made it clear to his hosts that the college would be an ideal place for him to research and write up his ideas. Back in Ardleigh, he suggested to Phyl that they take a holiday in the Aberystwyth area later in the summer.

As the local elections approached, he was asked to stand for election as a councillor in Ardleigh. He felt that his long-term support of the Labour Party would surprise and disappoint those who had asked him and declined with thanks. A month after the elections his decision was confirmed as the right one, by a letter from the principal of the Aberystwyth College of Librarianship. The principal expressed his delight at the stimulating lecture Mac had given and suggested two possibilities for further involvement. One possibility was the publication of a series of longer articles in the *Journal of Library Studies.* The editor would be keen to discuss such a project with him. The other suggestion, which the principal would put to the governors, if Mac were to agree, was the offer of full-time employment in which, in return for a few hours lecturing or seminar work, Mac could undertake the studies and writing that interested him. The contract could run for a term, or even a year, and the resultant work could almost certainly be published under the college imprint.

Mac showed the letter to Phyl. "It's a fantastic opportunity," he said, "but only if you are happy about it."

"Of course you must take it," she said. "It's what you've wanted from the time you left Tottenham. You'll never forgive yourself, or me, if you don't take it."

"But you're so settled here. I've never seen you so contented. And then there's the problem of the house. We'd have to sell it and find somewhere in Aberystwyth. It is a real shame, so soon after we've become so settled."

"Arch, you've got to do it. You know you have. I don't want to move, but if that's what we have to do, I expect I'll get used to it."

"Well, why don't we go over to Aberystwyth for a few days at the end of the month? Get a better idea of the place."

"As long as it's a bit of a holiday; I don't want to be left on my own for hours while you spend all the time talking libraries."

Mac replied by return of post, expressing his enthusiastic interest in the idea of a year's employment, but pointing out the problem of selling and buying houses. He suggested some part-time employment after the year and informed the principal of their proposed visit. The principal was delighted by Mac's positive response. The talks went well and a formal interview was arranged for 14th August. As a result of the interview and a subsequent medical examination, Mac was offered the post of research assistant on the maximum point of the Lecturer Grade 1 scale, £1,735 per annum. He accepted the offer and the search for a house began in earnest.

During his visits to Aberystwyth, Mac had developed a friendship with the warden of Tanybwlch Hall of Residence. The warden had made him most welcome and, once the appointment was confirmed, had helped him find a suitable house. At the end of September in 1969, Mac signed the contract for Rosemount, a two-storey house in Llanon, a small town a few miles south of Aberystwyth on the Cardiganshire coast. He took up his appointment from 27th October, but spent the first few weeks at Tanybwlch Hall, until the house was suitable to move into.

Back in Ardleigh on her own, Phyl was feeling increasingly concerned as news from Kenya, both in the press and in Keith's weekly letters, described the violence in Kisumu as President Kenyatta's bodyguards opened fire on the crowd that had gathered at the ceremonial opening of the new Russian hospital. One of Keith's colleagues was arrested for breaching the curfew which had been imposed following the troubles. There had also been a number of violent raids on the Yala compound and elsewhere in the locality. Fortunately, the curfew led to the arrest of the perpetrators but this didn't stop Phyl from worrying. Arch was away during the week both lecturing and sorting out the house in Llanon. In early December of 1969 he was unwell. He had been working on the house, but at the same time getting used to college life and trying to sell the Ardleigh house.

In the New Year, Phyl was further worried by a letter from Keith which described a leopard roaming the school compound during the night. What concerned Mac more were the arrangements when Keith and his family came home on leave in April. The plan was for them to live in the downstairs flat at Llanon, but it was neither decorated nor furnished, and the Ardleigh house had still not sold. In addition, Keith was suggesting that Mac should buy them a car for use over their leave and meet them at the airport along with Carol's parents. Keith said that their friends from Harlow would deliver some of the furniture they had stored during their absence. Over the Easter term Mac lived a Spartan existence in Llanon, but had more time for his own research and writing. Towards the end of March, the Ardleigh house was sold and Phyl could finally move up to Llanon in time for the family leave in April.

Rosemount was an interesting house, built on a steep hillside. The top storey, in which Arch and Phyl lived, appeared to be a bungalow from the front entrance. It had a spacious kitchen and lounge, as well as a bedroom with en-suite bathroom. Downstairs, which from the entrance appeared the lower storey of the house, formed a separate flat which, by the time Arch had completed a refit and redecoration, provided very attractive accommodation. Arch's aim was to have the flat ready for Keith's family when they came home on leave. This was achieved and Carol, in particular, was impressed by the style of decoration as well as the provision of facilities. Phyl was thrilled to have the grandchildren around and amused by their antics. She was reassured by their energy and seemingly good health. All too soon they were off again and safely back in their school by the end of August.

***

In the autumn of 1970, Mac had a message from former colleagues at Tottenham to say that his old friend and colleague, Walter Preston, was retiring as acting director in Haringey. Mac had known Walter since their schooldays. He had welcomed him into Tottenham as a trainee and later, after Mac himself had returned to Tottenham as director, he had welcomed Walter again as he rejoined the staff after war service. From then on they had worked closely throughout Mac's directorship. As he was unable to attend the farewell presentation, Mac recorded a taped message of appreciation and gratitude for their time together and wished him a long and happy retirement. Walter and his wife, Marjorie, remained good friends with Archie and Phyl for the rest of their lives.

In Llanon, Archie and Phyl joined the Anglo-Welsh Society in an effort to integrate into the local community. They found that the society membership was almost entirely composed of English people, who for one reason or another, had settled in the area. Phyl was amazed by local neighbours who said that as they were Welsh they did not need to join the society, they already knew Welsh ways and the local area. Archie and Phyl enjoyed the meetings, nevertheless, and made some new friends.

Phyl became seriously worried about the grandchildren again when they received a letter saying that Lee had had to have an emergency operation for a twisted intestine. There had clearly been difficulties at the hospital, which fortunately had been overcome. In due course he was home, fully recovered. All Phyl's old fears had been revived and she waited impatiently for their return to England, and Wales.

***

From January to March of 1971 there was a postal strike, which meant that Arch and Phyl heard nothing from the family in Kenya. The exchange of letters soon resumed but there was nothing untoward until June, when Lisa went into hospital to have her tonsils removed. Phyl was as worried as ever, but Lisa was soon home and well.

Arch and Phyl returned to Ardleigh over the Easter break to visit their friends there. Back at college, Arch had more time to concentrate on his writing, as most of the courses he had been lecturing for were complete. In the summer vacation, he was able to work again on the lower flat, with a view to renting it out, and by the end of September he was able to advertise it, to considerable interest. Arch had second thoughts. Maybe they should sell it. Keith showed some interest but it would depend where he found a job when they returned. In the meantime, Keith's family had a move to Kisumu confirmed. Keith would now be head of English at Kisumu Girls' High School from January and the family would live in the town. As both children were now of school age and Carol was teaching in the primary school, it seemed the logical move for the last eighteen months of their tour.

"They're going to stay out there even longer now," said Phyl, holding the blue airmail letter in her hand. "His handwriting doesn't get any better."

"How much longer?" asked Mac.

"Till July next year."

"Well, that does make sense if he's going to teach back here; as long as he gets a job to start in September. What else does he say?"

"They like their new bungalow and they don't miss Yala."

"I suppose it's much easier for Carol, now they live in the town."

Family correspondence continued on the usual regular basis until another three-week strike towards the end of February in 1972. In the meantime, Mac described the redecoration of the downstairs flat that he was currently engaged in.

In March, Mac was ill for three weeks and had to see a specialist at the hospital. The following month he was involved in a car accident but escaped unhurt. He returned to work at the end of May. He was still short of time to write as a result of lecturing commitments. Keith's contract extension to July was confirmed and he told them of plans to apply for Further Education work abroad.

"When are we going to get to know our grand-children?" said Phyl. "Surely they can come home after all these years."

"Well, I've sent him the leaflets on the Wimpey housing he asked for, so they must have some thoughts about coming home," said Mac.

"They seem to have so many accidents and horrible diseases. The sooner they bring those poor little things home the better. It's all very well for them to say it's nothing to worry about."

"I'm sure they're all right." said Mac, "They obviously care for them. You could tell how good they were with them when they came home on leave."

"That was here at home," said Phyl. "That's completely different."

In the new year both father and son were working on their books. Keith was hoping to have his play published, as it had done quite well at the schools' drama festival in Nairobi, but after a rejection from one publisher it was included in a group of plays for schools and published by Longman. Mac was at last making good progress with his book, *The Reader, the Library and the Book*. Clive Bingley published it during 1973.

Keith and Carol were still uncertain about their plans from July, but in May Keith came back to England for some job interviews. He managed to visit Carol's parents in Loughborough and spend a day and a night in Llanon. He returned to Kenya with a post as head of English at The Hurst School, in the north of Hampshire between Basingstoke and Reading. Phyl was greatly relieved. He's seen sense at last, she thought. There was one more surprise before the family came home.

Phyl answered a knock on the door to see an African couple standing there. A taxi was just driving away.

"Good afternoon, Mrs McClellan, my name is Denis and this is my wife, Jane. We are on a study tour from Kenya. I was a colleague of your son, who gave me your address so that we could stay for a few days."

"You had better come in," said Phyl. All she could think of was how black they were.

"They asked us on the bus," said Jane, "asked us if we had any contacts here. Keith had given us your address and told us to look you up if we had a chance. So here we are." She smiled shyly.

Phyl offered them a cup of tea and showed them to the flat downstairs. "Make yourselves at home," she said, and returned upstairs.

"We've got visitors," she said when Mac came in, "I've told them when dinner is. They're downstairs," she said, "in the flat."

Mac chatted with Denis about Yala and was delighted by how much respect he obviously had for Keith. He was also able to give Denis considerable help with his studies and they set off together in the morning, leaving Jane with Phyl. The two women got on from the beginning. Phyl was fascinated by Jane's experiences as a nurse in Kenya and delighted by her lively open friendliness. She couldn't help noticing how much more freely she spoke than when Denis was with her. Her whole demeanour was so different when no men were present. After a few days, when the group moved on, Denis and Jane offered heartfelt thanks. Back in Kenya they told Keith they had been so grateful. They had been made to feel as if they were in their own home. Denis gave Keith some money with which to buy a present to show their gratitude.

Keith asked Mac to find him details of estate agents in Basingstoke. In response, Mac sent him a file of house details and estate agents in the area. By the end of July they were all packed and they flew home on 2nd August. On the very same day, the play that Keith had written and directed was shown on Kenya TV for the first time. Their arrival coincided with the three-day week and the fuel shortage. Their new Skoda Octavia was waiting for them at Heathrow, but the tyres were flat. Nevertheless they were soon back in Llanon and settling into the downstairs flat, which was now completely redecorated. Phyl was thrilled to see the grandchildren and impressed with how they had grown. Keith and Carol began a rapid house search, and settled on an older three-storey house in Thatcham; about six miles from the school. They could not move in until just before Christmas, so Keith spent the weekdays at a hostel for workers at the nuclear site in Aldermaston and came home to Carol and the children at weekends. The children went to the local primary school, where all lessons were in Welsh. This did hold back their education, but at least Phyl could spend lots of time with them.

Chapter Fifteen

Retirement

"He was a man of honesty and humour; a man of integrity and compassion. He was a good man and his going has left emptiness."

At the college Mac taught courses in aspects of librarianship, but also had time to develop his ideas by drawing together aspects of theory and practice he had developed throughout his own career, but augmented by the ideas and writings of others. In the introduction to *The Reader, the Library and the Book*, which was eventually published by Clive Bingley Ltd in 1973, he wrote that *the increasing application of management techniques to the administration of local services, including the use of independent teams to assess the effectiveness of the use of resources, obliges the librarian to be clear as to his objectives and to be in a position to justify his use of resources.* He goes on to make a prescient point about the future influence of *sophisticated audio-retrieval systems and of computer-based information retrieval.*

Just as the plan he had drawn up at the outset of his directorship at Tottenham, in 1946, had stated, he wrote that *The key theme is the conviction that purpose, and the objectives which will achieve purpose, must derive from the understanding that the library is part of the total system of communication operating within society, and from the individual and social implications of the reading activity itself.* Mac went on to say that this definition of purpose posed a number of questions. The chapters of his book were an exploration of many of these questions. They were largely the updating of articles he had written for various library publications and conferences, and were based on the practical applications he had introduced in Tottenham.

After discussions at a meeting of the department of administrative studies, Mac was prompted to offer a memorandum[156] on a revised organisational structure for the college. He applied the same principles as he had in the reorganisation at Tottenham, in that he proposed that the administrative duties be managed and structured separately from the academic departments. He gave a detailed structural plan which was welcomed by the various relevant officers. A number of problems with his plan were identified but the principles were accepted and the clarity of his thinking appreciated.

While Mac was updating his theories of the various aspects of librarianship

---

156 Memorandum re future structure of the college. AWM 1.10.71

through his lectures, papers for professional publications and the production of *The Reader, the Library and the Book*, he was researching and developing methods of book stock control. In the book he devotes a long chapter to this aspect of his work, and he continued to consult on and research the subject[157].

He identifies two aspects of book provision. There is the bibliographical aspect for which librarians require professional knowledge and experience. A librarian will develop a detailed knowledge of books of a particular subject area, or group of connected areas. This will include the full range from introductory, more general works to more detailed academic studies, and an awareness of the accessibility of such books, whether on the shelves, in reserve or only available through the sharing system. As the *Service in Depth* system in Tottenham had demonstrated, professional librarians with such expertise should be available to advise readers for, as Mac said, "You wouldn't expect a doctor to tell you to look up your problem in an *Excerpta Medica*".

The second aspect of book provision, and one Mac felt had been largely neglected, was the logistics. This involves the correct distribution between fields of literature in accordance with the varying needs of readers. This, in turn, requires the maximisation of reader accessibility to books, with the minimisation in the deterioration of the book stock. The system should also avoid subjective discrimination against individuals or groups of readers. All this must be delivered within the overall resources available.

Whilst the bibliographical aspect could only be addressed through individual books and readers, the logistical task is to stock books likely to have greatest use and perfect the machinery for obtaining those books for which potential use is below shelf space allowance. The stock should be grouped in a series of interest categories. Manually, the librarian could manage about 150 categories, but far more could be managed on a computer.

The next calculation is to decide what proportion of shelf space would be the most efficient for each category. Equal proportions would not work, as clearly some categories are more popular, and have more titles, than others. The answer Mac proposed was the recording of loans by category on a particular day to represent the current use by the readership. The square roots of each total should then be calculated, the results added together and the percentage of the total that each square root represents becomes that category's share of the shelf space. As readership of categories is subject to change, the numbers should be recalculated four times a year.

---

157 McClellan, A.W. *The Reader, the Library and the Book,* ch8 pp83-105

The next factor Mac considered was the causes and rates of stock depreciation and the calculation of replacement rates. He developed formulae to cover wear and tear, the bibliographical need for new updated editions, and the fact that in some smaller categories a reader may have read all the books. He also made allowance for over or under provision in certain categories in previous years. From all these factors, Mac proposed that the annual book fund that the library needed to maintain and update the book stock could be calculated.

Mac was in enthusiastic discussion with a senior lecturer at the Librarianship Department of Leeds Polytechnic over the number of bibliographical groups that should be used for stock management. He was excited by the prospects that computerisation might offer, although he felt his own direct involvement in this new technology was a step too far for his own work. His thinking on these issues was published as *The Logistics of a Public Library Bookstock* in 1978.

Mac retired from the college in 1975, but continued to write and research as he felt there was so much more to do, as with the stock control issues described above. In 1973, he was honoured for his outstanding contribution to the literature of librarianship when he was elected a Fellow of the Library Association.[158] In June 1974, he attended a residential conference of the International and Comparative Reading Library Group at Middleton Hall, Corebridge, Scotland. Here he delivered a well received paper, entitled *Comparative Reading – A Librarian's View.*

As his time at the college drew to a close, he received a Christmas card from his students, thanking him for his kindness to them during their time at the College of Librarianship, Wales.

"We can move away from here now," said Phyl. "I don't really like it here. As I keep saying, they don't really want us here, most of the locals."

"We've made some friends," said Mac.

"English people, yes, but the atmosphere's not welcoming. Not like it was in Ardleigh."

"I was thinking we could go over there for a few days. See how things are. Check house prices and so on."

After a week or so tidying up his paperwork and leaving the college for the last time, Mac drove them over to Ardleigh. They were welcomed by

158 (Admin/Biographical History – Archives Hub, Thomas Parry Library, Dept of Libraries and information studies, Aberystwyth.) p 2 of 6.

their friends, but Mac was horrified to discover that, whereas when they had moved, Rosemount had been almost the same price as the Ardleigh house, if local prices were any guide Ardleigh was now twice as expensive. They drove back to Rosemount feeling quite depressed.

"Perhaps there is somewhere we can afford nearer the grandchildren," said Phyl.

"Let's get this house on the market and get a better idea of prices," said Mac. "And I'll look for areas where prices are more reasonable. No point in getting too close to Keith and Carol, though. He'll want to change his job in due course, and they could go anywhere."

They stayed with their son and his family a number of times in 1975, partly to search for a suitable house. Mac became very frustrated by the situation. There was no interest shown in Rosemount and he could not make up his mind about where he wanted to live. His frustration continued through the next two years. The estate agents did little to promote the sale and no sign was displayed. In November 1977 Mac fell and broke his arm. He was unable to drive for about ten weeks. At Christmas they took the train to Swindon where Keith collected them and brought them to Thatcham for the usual few days, with Carol's parents also there.

In March 1978, a neighbour told Mac that his son's family were looking for a house. He asked if they could look at Rosemount. It proved ideal and they could not understand why the estate agent had not given them the details. With a sale now likely, their search for a house for their own move became urgent. Mac considered several possibilities but finally settled on a house in Trowbridge in Wiltshire. In June they moved to a pleasant house in Avonvale Lane, Trowbridge. At much the same time, Keith was appointed deputy head at the John O'Gaunt School in Hungerford.

Once they were settled in Trowbridge they made friends with nearby couples. Mac joined the local Probus group and enjoyed the conversations at the long lunches. In the autumn he joined a carpentry class and began to produce a range of furniture pieces. By 1980 he had produced desks for his grandchildren, and the frame for a grandfather clock in which he fitted the workings which set and balanced perfectly. He made a number of cupboards and other furniture for their own home and delighted Keith and Carol when he presented them with an inlaid chess board coffee table with a set of chess pieces. He also tried carving small wooden sculptures, including a cat which seemed to flow with motion.

Mac and Phyl continued to see Keith's family more regularly than they had when they lived at Rosemount. When Carol's father had a heart attack in November 1982, they were able to drive over to Thatcham at short notice to look after the grandchildren while Carol and Keith went up to Loughborough to support her mother and visit Reg in hospital. Reg's health varied after his initial recovery so he and Eve missed Christmas at Thatcham that year.

In March 1983, Mac and Phyl celebrated their Golden Wedding with a dinner at the Beach Arms Hotel in Basingstoke. Mac had gone through his usual worries about where and how to celebrate, but with the dinner and Carol's Golden Wedding cake the celebration was enjoyed by everyone. Only two months later Phyl had a heart attack. She seemed to recover reasonably well and Christmas that year was celebrated with Keith and Carol and Reg and Eve as usual. In February 1984 Phyl had a stroke. Keith and Carol came to visit. Phyl seemed confused but Mac did not call a doctor as it was the weekend. By the time the doctor arrived, Phyl was paralysed down one side and could not speak. She was very confused. She was taken to hospital in Bath and never emerged except for brief visits, until after Mac's death, when she was moved to a care home in Newbury so that Keith could visit regularly.

Mac was traumatised by Phyl's illness. Keith and Carol came over every weekend for the next month and prepared lunch and cleaned the house. A month later Mac had a severe attack of bronchitis. His sister Joyce and her husband came to stay and looked after him. Once he had recovered, he came over to Thatcham to stay with Keith and Carol for a few days and then he went on holiday to Cornwall with the whole family. He seemed to have recovered and was more cheerful, especially with the grandchildren. He met their friends and called on his sister-in-law, Rita. Her husband, Mac's brother Stuart, had recently died. Stuart and Rita had moved to Bodmin soon after the Second World War, where they had bought and run the Royal Hotel.

From then on, Keith and Carol visited Trowbridge every other weekend. Carol would cook lunch and bring some of Mac's favourite cakes, and Keith would do some housework or some gardening. On the weekends in between, Mac would drive over to Thatcham for lunch. Towards the end of August, Keith and Carol and the children moved to Monks Lane in Newbury, but the fortnightly arrangements continued. In mid-November Mac was taken into Trowbridge Hospital with a blocked lung. The problem was diagnosed as lung cancer and chemotherapy was organised. Mac knew he was at risk of dying and became very depressed. After a week, Keith came to collect him from the hospital in Bath to which he had been transferred. He spent a few days in Newbury and walked down to the shops with Keith, but he was quite weak and was sick several times. He was worried about leaving Phyl. He had a forlorn hope that she may recover enough to come home to live. An end-of-life care worker visited and talked him through all that he needed to do and what he would face. He felt some relief from her visit.

Keith brought him over to stay for a few days two or three times leading up to Christmas and his mood varied. By Christmas he was very weak. Keith brought his parents to spend Christmas with them. Mac had hoped to be able to manage Phyl by helping her in and out of bed and with dressing and washing but he found he could not. He went into the bathroom after every meal and made himself sick. Keith took him back to Trowbridge and Phyl back to hospital on Boxing Day.

In the new year he was clearly very ill. The doctor gave him six months at most. In the second week in January when Keith and Carol visited, he was clearly too ill to cope. They called the doctor and were told to take him to the hospital. He was very depressed again. His sister Joyce and her husband came to be with him. Keith and Carol were under more pressure as Carol's mother had fallen seriously ill in Loughborough. Mac was moved into a hospice at the beginning of February. On 6th February, Keith and Carol were called to the hospice. Phyl sat in her wheelchair, tears flowing freely. Mac was unconscious but tossing and turning restlessly, clinging to his beloved duvet. By late afternoon, Phyl could no longer cope. Keith drove her back to the hospital. Later they were told that Mac would not recover consciousness but would pass away in the next few hours. They said their goodbyes and drove back to Newbury. At 1.30 am on 7th February 1985, Mac died.

At his funeral in the Bath cemetery chapel, the vicar read the eulogy which Keith had written.

Born into a humble but loving family, Mac worked hard from an early age to educate himself for a place in the world to reflect his abilities and interests. He found it in the profession of librarianship, in which he had a long and distinguished career. His was a major contribution to the theory and practice of librarianship in the post-war years. Through his love of peace and the democratic freedoms, he pursued the opening up of man's creativity and knowledge through the medium of the public library service. Yet, exciting though his ideas were, his colleagues and students loved and respected him as much for his humour, compassion and friendship, as for his professional excellence.

In the home he was a craftsman with a flair for creativity and design. He enjoyed tackling problems with persistence and ingenuity and took proper satisfaction in their solution.

As a family man he was a wonderful husband and father. He attributed his successful career very largely to the love and support of his wife, Phyllis, whom he loved and cherished through almost fifty-two years of marriage. He was not just a loving father to his family, but a loving friend who sustained, supported and shared their lives through setbacks and successes.

He gave friendship and love with confidence, but without affectation. He held back no kindness through fear of recrimination or the appearance of weakness.

He was a man of honesty and humour; a man of integrity and compassion. He was a good man and his going has left an emptiness.

Many letters of condolence arrived from friends and work colleagues and both his former deputies at Tottenham wrote detailed obituaries in the Library Association Journal.

Epilogue

"McClellan's theories were in advance of the means by which they could achieve their full potential in practice." Wendy Spinks.

What lasting impact did McClellan's library scheme have? He recognised that it had faults and difficulties and he was always looking for improvements. He wrote that computers could be of great assistance in a number of ways but particularly in stock control logistics. He acknowledged that initially the scheme could well produce potential stock provision at great variance with current stock. The librarian would need a firm commitment to introduce the scheme.

The reorganisation of local government provided an opportunity for the adoption of such a scheme but it was largely ignored. As Wendy Spinks points out, although librarians were new to computers, and waited to see what they could do and how to use them, McClellan was thinking about this twenty years previously. Thus the spread of his ideas was almost entirely limited to those who had worked with him. Philip Colehan introduced a slightly modified form of the system in Hillingdon; A. G. Enser adopted a version modified to suit the central library in Eastbourne, and Ken Jones propounded the advantages of the system in relation to management theory at Leeds University.

Versions of the *Service in Depth* system of shelving and layout were adopted quite widely from the outset and modern libraries are arranged in ways that are directly developed from Mac's original scheme. Bradford and Luton were early converts to a basic version of the scheme.

Mac thought that the integration of reference and home reading stock was useful for medium-sized libraries, but less so for large ones where the stretch of books on a particular subject could become unwieldy. At Bedford, the idea that children's non-fiction for the over nines should be integrated with the adult section was introduced. The intention was to encourage the development of a family centred library. A variation was introduced at Oxford, where reference books were put at the end of appropriate subject shelving bays.

Hillingdon operated a simplified form of stock control from 1968. A working party of librarians divided the stock into two hundred interest categories. Quarterly counts of the issue were taken and the square root of the highest recorded issue was used to produce the target stock figure of that category. The system met with some staff resistance as there seemed a lot of work for comparatively little return. Computerisation of the system would relieve the workload that manual collection and calculation demanded. A number of libraries showed interest and instigated some research by counting issues in various interest groups, but these were one-off schemes.

In the late seventies, another librarian was working on similar lines to Mac in improving stock control. George Kerr only came to hear of Mac in the mid nineties. While at a conference in North Carolina, Kerr met a well-known German librarian, Ute Klaassen, who had also worked at stock control on very similar lines. It seems all three librarians independently developed a methodology based on similar principles. Mac would have loved to work with them if only he had known of their work. Eventually computerisation took stock control away from librarians at local libraries into centralised cataloguing. In the mid 1990s, George Kerr developed a system called Evidence Based Stock Management[159]. The system, which is now widely used in libraries across the world, has adopted the basic principles of Mac's theory. It aims to provide quality and relevance to the collection of stock. It does so by monitoring collection supply against collection demand. It also removes worn out or unused books, but there is no direct indication of how shelf space is calculated.

Recent cuts in public library services have led to a great reduction in qualified librarians able to advise readers in bibliographic detail. The large number of volunteers now essential to the continuing provision of the service is testimony to the strong desire of many to see the service continue. As Mac stated in his original plan for Tottenham and reiterated during his broadcast in 1950, the public library is an essential element of communication which uniquely offers the reader access to the widest range of ideas, opinions and theories through uncensored provision. As such it should be defended and supported throughout these difficult times and beyond.

Mac was a true pioneer in the philosophy and practice of public libraries. His ideas were effective because he developed efficient and cost-effective methods of implementing them, and was able to earn the support of his staff through consulting them and taking their interests into account throughout the process. He was a strong supporter of education and thence of children's libraries and schools and young people's provision in museums. Yet, though consumed by enthusiasm and determination to achieve his plans at work, he was still a wonderful and at times delightfully eccentric husband, father and wider family man.

---

159 G. Kerr, Update 5 dec2006 pp34-5

Acknowledgements

I have had tremendous support from a wide range of people in producing this biography. These include: the archivists at Tower Hamlets, Bromley, Chelmsford and, above all, at Bruce Castle, Haringey; the librarians of the Thomas Parry Library, University of Wales, Aberystwyth; the University of Sussex for free access to the Mass Observation report on Reading in Tottenham. Wendy Spinks for donating a copy of her dissertation on 'A consideration of attempts to relate public library stock to user needs, with particular reference to the ideas of A.W. McClellan, and current library practice in the London Borough of Haringey'. Philip Colehan for sharing memories of working with Mac, and George Kerr, for responding with useful detail about the work he did with the help of Ute Klaassen. O.U.D.C.E. course tutors, Nick Kneale, now deceased, and Dr Sarah Burton for their guidance, support and encouragement; Amanda Leigh, for her supportive copy-editing. Members of several writing groups have read and advised me with great patience. In particular, Brian Reynolds, Peter Norris, Frank Vielba, all of whom have given detailed advice on the text. Many other friends have read and commented on various sections of the text and I am grateful to them all. I must also acknowledge the continuing patience and support of my wife, Carol, who cared for and loved my father when he was alive and has been a source of many fond memories, either directly, or through her detailed diaries kept over many of the relevant years.

Photographs:

Poplar Library and R101 over Poplar, by kind permission of Tower Hamlets Library and Archive Department.

Bromley Local Studies and Archives: Penge Public Library, 194 Anerley Road.

Chelmsford Emergency Information Centre 1940-45, Pictorial Press.

Haringey Archives: Director and Vera Brittain, 2 Mobile Library pictures, Coronation Proclamation.

Getty Images: No More War Demonstration 1924.

About the Author

Much of Keith McClellan's early life is described in the text and needs no expansion. During his time in Kenya he wrote and directed plays, which were performed at The National Theatre of Kenya in Nairobi. One of these was published by Longman and Keith directed it on Kenyan television. Later, as head of a comprehensive school in Oxfordshire, he published articles in the local press and The Times Educational Supplement. In retirement he took up writing, broadcast a piece on Radio Oxford, performed his work with colleagues at Oxford Fringe festivals and published a novel, *The Bootlegger's Widow*. He gives talks to interested groups on creative writing to publication. He is married with two adult children and two grandchildren.